# Keeping in Touch

*Christian Formation and Teaching*

## Carol F. Krau

**DISCIPLESHIP** RESOURCES

P.O. BOX 840 • NASHVILLE, TENNESSEE 37202-0840

www.discipleshipresources.org

Cover design and book design by Lori Haley

ISBN 0-88177-248-8

Library of Congress Catalog Card No. 98-86153

DR248

# TABLE OF CONTENTS

# PREFACE

There are two things I really, really love to do: (1) I love to teach; and (2) I love to work with other adults who are teachers. One of my first teaching experiences was with my brother's fifth grade Sunday school class at Eastland Road United Methodist Church in Atlanta, Georgia. One of my most recent experiences was serving as a substitute teacher for the John Wesley Class at Belle Meade United Methodist Church in Nashville, Tennessee. That class was the first one organized in the church; the members have studied together for approximately forty years.

No matter the age group, no matter the location, no matter how short or how long the teaching assignment, I just love to teach! I can't imagine why there aren't people beating down the doors of the church and begging to teach. However, that doesn't appear to be the case in most of our congregations. In fact, the exact opposite is closer to reality in many United Methodist congregations today.

Since joining the staff of the General Board of Discipleship of The United Methodist Church, the question I have been asked most often by Sunday school superintendents, education committee members, and church staff has been, How do we get teachers? The second most frequent question is related to the first, How do we equip our teachers to be effective when there are so many demands on them in other arenas of their lives?

As I tried to respond to the questions, I began to realize that I was assuming a prior question. It seemed to me that before we can identify people with the gifts for teaching, we need to answer the question, What do we hope to accomplish in our teaching and learning? We also need a comprehensive picture of the teaching role. We've been "doing church" for so long that most of us assume that we all know what we're trying to accomplish and how we should get there. I think it's time to test our assumptions.

This book is written in response to my prior question. It is written out of a deep commitment to the vital role teaching plays in the formation of Christian disciples. It is also written out of a deep conviction that the way we've always done things isn't cutting it anymore. We live in a time of radical change. The Christian church no longer finds itself as the legitimizer and norm-setter for our society. Mainline denominations have suffered significant losses in membership over the past several decades. Many people are turning to "non-traditional" sources of spirituality. If the Christian church is to be relevant (as well as prophetic) in today's culture, we must change the way we teach and learn.

Much of what has been written in other resources about teaching deals with the theory and theology of religious education. If a book is specifically for teachers, the content often focuses on specific lesson plans or teaching methods. What differentiates this resource from others is that it is an attempt to articulate a framework for understanding the breadth of the teaching role called for by the changing circumstances in which we find ourselves. It focuses on habits and practices that teachers need to develop and strengthen in order to create environments that shape people as Christian disciples. It is not as much a how-to book as it is a what-if resource.

Through this resource I hope to invite teachers, pastors, and other educational leaders to engage in the study and reflection necessary for building effective systems of teaching and learning in their congregations. The time of top-down programming is over. The time for dialogue and partnership is here. If this resource facilitates dialogue and strengthens partnership, it will have served its purpose.

I am well aware of the limitations of this resource. Over the past year I have gone to bed many nights with books such as *Devotional Life in the Wesleyan Tradition* and *The Learning Congregation: A New Vision of Leadership*. I still feel sure that tomorrow I will find the exact book I needed to read to make this a more thorough and helpful resource. However, the time for closure has come, if only to stay in the good graces of my editor, Deb Smith.

I would like to express my appreciation to the many teachers and Christian educators across the country who have heard me explain bits and pieces of theories and concepts that eventually grew into this book. Your feedback was invaluable.

I would also like to thank my team members for their continual support, for their friendship, and for their amazing Christian witness. Marigene, Anne, Bill, Shirley, JoAnn, Mary, and Blanca, you are a blessing to me. I am grateful to Ezra Earl Jones, who met with me during the early conceptual stages of this book. His insight into the significance of the early Methodist class meetings helped me clarify some of the crucial issues and focus the direction of the book. And I owe Donna Gaither big-time for her patience and her sense of humor. We started out to write a book together, but I kept changing directions on her. In her great wisdom she finally told me to write the book myself. Our conversations may have been frustrating for Donna, but they were instrumental in crystallizing the concepts and content for me.

Finally, I want to express my abiding love and gratitude to the four people who are my primary teachers of the faith: my husband, Stephen, and our children, Vanessa, Jeremy, and Timothy. Your willingness to laugh with me, cry with me, confront me, and grow with me is a constant source of joy. Through you I see into the heart of God. And in response to your question, "Aren't you finished with that book yet?" the answer is "Yes. Glory to the Father! Hallelujah!"

# chapter 1

# TEACHING AS INCARNATION

*I am the vine, you are the branches. Those who abide in me and I in them bear much fruit, because apart from me you can do nothing....As the Father has loved me, so I have loved you; abide in my love.*

John 15:5, 9

"Take care of yourself. Keep in touch." How many times have you ended your correspondence or a conversation with these words? The phrase *keep in touch* is one way we express what it means to maintain healthy, significant relationships. Being *in touch* with someone commonly means being attuned to the nuances, expressions, moods, and behaviors of another person. In the same way, being *out of touch* is a derogatory assessment of someone who doesn't seem to understand what's going on.

Jesus was in touch with the people around him. Think for a moment about the stories of Jesus and Zacchaeus (Luke 19:1-10); Jesus and the Samaritan woman (John 4:7-42); Jesus and the lame man (John 5:2-9); Jesus and the children (Mark 10:13-16); and Jesus, Mary, and Martha (Luke 10:38-42). Each of these stories, as well as countless others, illustrates the particular way in which Jesus related to each person he met. He seemed to know exactly what each person needed, and he responded according to her or his need.

Jesus was also in touch with God. From the stories of his temptation in the wilderness immediately after his baptism to the account of his vigil in the garden of Gethsemane just prior to his arrest, trial, and crucifixion, the Scriptures witness to the frequency with which Jesus withdrew for prayer. These regular interludes for communion with God enabled Jesus to keep in touch with God's will for his life, his ministry, and, ultimately, his death and resurrection.

This book draws on the image of *keeping in touch* as a metaphor for a teaching style that anticipates sacred space in which people encounter the presence of the living God. It is written out of the belief that when teachers and learners are in touch with God and with one another, they experience the transforming power of God and learn to live as faithful disciples. This experience is rooted in the New Testament concept of incarnation, the understanding that God was present (incarnate) in human form in Jesus Christ.

As Christians, we believe that Jesus revealed the nature of God, the life and power of God, and the redemptive activity of God. When we read the Gospels, we come to understand God's nature as self-giving love. The power of God's righteousness, as revealed in Jesus of Nazareth, is able to transform human brokenness and alienation, restoring relationships between God and humanity and human beings with one another.

In the incarnation we begin to understand that doing God's will, which is the signpost of the kingdom of God, is a matter of love— loving God and loving neighbor. As we learn to abide in God's love and obey Jesus' commandment to love one another, we keep in touch with God and with one another. As we abide in God's love, we learn to acknowledge our own hurts, needs, struggles, gifts, and graces.

Teaching and learning for faithful discipleship have been a significant part of the church since its very beginning. Knowledge of the Scriptures, knowledge of the Christian faith, skills for participating in the church's mission—each are part of the content of the teaching ministry. Prayer, worship, awe, grace—these, too, are a part of the teaching ministry. Whenever God's people gather together, they claim the promise that God will be with them. And in some mysterious way God is indeed with them, and they are never again the same. When children, youth, and adults commit themselves to learning together, they can be assured of God's transforming power working in their midst.

That sounds wonderful, doesn't it? When it works, it is wonderful! It's amazing! In fact, I can't think of any other experience that compares with that of true Christian community in which all people understand themselves to be created in God's image; all people are committed to supporting one another's growth in faith; and all people are empowered by God's Spirit to live in faithful response to God's grace.

The only problem is that the majority of our congregations no longer have in place structures and processes that support such transformational experiences. In the last half of this century, the teaching ministry has undergone radical change. Fewer and fewer adults consider themselves equipped to lead effective learning experiences. More and more congregations are unable to identify and equip the teachers they need for small groups. Fewer and fewer people participate in traditional Sunday school classes. Yet more and more people express a desire to know God and to explore their spirituality.

In 1990 Search Institute, a research organization in Minneapolis, published a detailed study that documented the state of Christian education in six mainline denominations, including The United Methodist Church. The purposes of the study included assessing the maturity of faith of youth and adults and identifying factors that promoted faith maturity. The study defined mature faith as the integration of vertical faith (one's relationship with God) and horizontal faith (one's concern for the welfare of other human beings). Mature faith was measured against thirty-eight traits, such as accepting God's love as unconditional, experiencing meaning and purpose in life, applying faith to political and social issues, seeking opportunities for spiritual growth, and devoting time and energy to promoting social justice and world peace.

Some of the results from the study indicated the following about United Methodists: Sixty-eight percent of the adults surveyed had trouble accepting salvation as God's gift. Sixty-five percent of the adults rarely or never encouraged someone to believe in Jesus Christ. Seventy-five percent of the adults never participated in working for social justice. Thirty-four percent of the adults reported spending ten hours or fewer per year in any Christian education activity.

Many books have been written since this study, seeking to address the issues identified by Search Institute. Yet the many telephone calls, letters, and visits I have received or made around the country continue to give evidence that, for the most part, our congregational systems for teaching and learning are in serious trouble.

This really isn't news to anyone. Any perfunctory review of Christian education literature over the past twenty-five years will provide you with more than enough information on the problems of the Sunday school, the church school, religious education, and all the other phases we've gone through in the last half of this century in teaching and learning. Therefore, I do not propose to add yet another treatise on what ails the Sunday school. Rather, this book is about the role of teachers in Christian spiritual formation.

If strong, healthy relationships that are centered in Christ are the heart of Christian community, then it is imperative that our congregations identify those people with the necessary abilities to build and maintain those kinds of relationships. We need to discern which people in our congregations are keeping in touch with God and with the people around them, for it is those people who have already discovered the powerful presence of God in their lives and are committed to growing as disciples who can mentor others in their relationships with God and within the faith community.

However, it is impossible to speak of the teaching role without looking at the purpose of teaching and learning. How can we continue to ask people to teach without first being clear about what we are trying to accomplish through our teaching ministry? If the teaching ministry has radically changed, then so must the role of teachers.

Only when we are in touch with God can we discern the directions in which we need to move. Only when we are in touch with the shifts taking place in our communities and congregations can we address these shifts in light of the gospel.

While this may seem elementary, I believe that we can no longer assume that everyone in our congregations is clear about the mission of the church and how teaching and learning connect to and support that mission. Unless we understand our mission, it is fruitless to focus on recruitment of teachers. Only when we are clear about the task before us can we begin to clearly identify the gifts and graces needed for effective leadership in small groups.

## TEACHING FOR TRANSFORMATION

Out of necessity, I will need to rehearse some of our history as a way of setting the scene. First, I will rely on Loren B. Mead's work in *The Once and Future Church: Reinventing the Congregation for a New Mission Frontier* (The Alban Institute, 1993) to describe how the church has evolved over time, as well as the various systems of education that emerged to meet the changing needs of the church. Second, I will focus on the purpose of teaching and learning as it relates to the primary task of the congregation. Finally, I will suggest five critical processes for teachers in the future as the church seeks to live out its mission.

### The Apostolic Era

Mead describes the period of the early church immediately after the life, death, and resurrection of Jesus as the "Apostolic" Era. It was characterized by powerful preaching, teaching, and healing by those who had lived with and followed Jesus. The Acts of the Apostles recounts the story of these men and women, who received the Holy Spirit on Pentecost and moved out to change their world in the name of Jesus.

At first the followers of Jesus continued to meet in the synagogue for prayer and study, as was their custom in Judaism. Teaching and learning was an essential element of community life. The apostles witnessed to what they had seen and heard. They repeated the stories of Jesus and his ministry. They told of his death and resurrection.

While the Scriptures testify that thousands of people responded to their message, we also know from the Scriptures and from other historical writings that the political, social, and religious authorities were adamantly opposed to their preaching and teaching. Their antagonism toward these early followers of Christianity erupted into violence, persecution, and dispersion.

In light of the hostile environment in which the church found itself, the believers came to understand mission as right outside their doors. Each person they met was a potential candidate for baptism, faith, and incorporation into the body of Christ.

This early community of faith had to depend on each other. They spent much time together praying, studying the Scriptures, sharing in the Lord's Supper, and caring for the needs of the community. "With great power the apostles gave their testimony to the resurrection of the Lord Jesus, and great grace was upon them all" (Acts 4:33).

As their numbers increased, the apostles invited the community of faith to discern those people with the gifts and graces for leadership. Deacons were appointed to share in the task of administration and serving the various needs of the community, particularly those of the widows. Each believer was needed in order for the community to function properly. Each believer understood that God had called him or her to discipleship. And "with glad and generous hearts," they praised God and experienced the "goodwill of all the people" (Acts 2:46-47).

## The Christendom Era

With the conversion of Emperor Constantine, the Apostolic Era came to an end. As you will remember from world history class, Christianity became the favored religion of the Roman Empire when Constantine became a Christian in A.D. 312.

As time went by, *citizens* became synonymous with *Christians* in the eyes of the political, religious, and social authorities. The society was no longer hostile to the church. Society embraced the church.

Mead describes this period of church history as the "Christendom" Era. As Christianity evolved into a legitimate religion, it was institutionalized and formalized. The Christendom Era gave birth to church professionals. Over time, the roles of clergy and laity became more distinct. Mission moved from one's doorstep to beyond the boundaries of the empire. Only special people called by God to preach to the "pagans" were involved in mission. And none of the laity needed to worry too much about their spiritual gifts, because everyone they knew was already a Christian.

In the past two hundred years the prevailing mode of teaching and learning in the institutional church has been the Sunday school. Begun in England in the 1780's by Robert Raikes, the Sunday school was organized to teach morals and manners to children of the poor. In the United States, once public school education became accessible to children, the Sunday school no longer had to teach reading and writing. Religious instruction became its main undertaking.

According to Robert W. Lynn and Elliott Wright, the Sunday school became a "how-to" movement with conversion as its goal during the nineteenth century (The Big Little School: 200 Years of the Sunday School; Abingdon Press, 1980). As such, it was a strong ally of the great revivals that swept through American Protestantism. Diverse denominations cooperated in establishing Sunday schools throughout the country. In order to meet this goal, they refused to address social or political issues facing the country.

The Sunday school was one of the few places where laity could provide significant leadership. Indeed, its very success depended on the overwhelming number of volunteers who served as teachers. At its heyday during the nineteenth century, the Sunday school boasted large attendance, national conventions, and, eventually, large denominational structures and staff to keep it operating.

Before the rise of the Sunday school, the Methodist movement had developed another process for growing in the faith. In the 1740's, John Wesley started class meetings, small groups that met weekly under the supervision of a class leader. These classes gathered for the purpose of supporting each other in living as Christian disciples.

The class meetings represented the practicality of Wesley's theology of discipleship. Wesley knew that human nature was "weak." He believed that the Christian community should support its members in the faith, rather than blaming them for failing to live up to the demands of the gospel.

Wesley's theology of discipleship was grounded in his doctrine of grace, which he described as prevenient grace, justifying grace, and sanctifying grace. Discipleship for Wesley was a balance between works of piety (personal devotion and communal worship) and works of mercy (personal compassion and corporate actions for justice).

Wesley believed that one's inward holiness of heart would lead to outward holiness in behavior. Good works were a sign of obedience. If prevenient grace was the working of God in human souls even before they were aware of it, and justifying grace was a gift of God leading to new birth, then sanctifying grace led to empowering human will for accountable discipleship. Class meetings provided men and women with the opportunity to grow in God's grace as they sought to be obedient to the will of God.

While the Sunday school developed, the tradition of the class meeting decreased in most European-American congregations. During the twentieth century, much of the Sunday school philosophy in mainline Protestant denominations has been a combination of progressive educational theory and liberal theology. Based on a schooling model that assumed one could learn during childhood everything needed to live successfully as an adult, the Sunday school has consisted primarily of closely graded classes of children (one or two ages in a class). The basic approach has been cognitive instruction in which adult teachers transmit information to children, youth, and other adults.

## The Post-Christendom Era

Much of the history of the church falls into the Christendom Era. It is only in our lifetime that this era has begun to collapse. We are now in an emerging post-Christendom Era. Because we are in the midst of the transition, we aren't sure exactly what this new epoch in church history will be.

At least one characteristic seems to be evident: At best, society is now indifferent to the church; at worst, it is again hostile. Being a citizen of the state is no longer considered synonymous with being a disciple of Jesus Christ. Nor should it be. No longer do social structures support the values and beliefs of the Christian faith. There is a great deal of controversy over the influence of religious beliefs in political policymaking. For the most part, religion is considered a private matter.

Inside, the church is no better. In assuming that everyone was a Christian, we felt no urgent need to support people's growth in faith. While we sent our children to Sunday school, we went to breakfast. Once our junior high children were confirmed, they were allowed to go to band or soccer practice on Sunday mornings. We now have a generation of adults with little biblical knowledge, little understanding of the rituals and symbols of the faith, little appreciation for the liturgy and worship of our congregations, little ability to articulate their beliefs, and little ability to reflect on their experiences in light of their faith.

What a time to be called to work in the church! I feel like praying an ancient prayer of the church that I used to hear my mother pray when she was upset: "Lord, have mercy on me, a poor sinner!" Yet with all my heart, I believe that God's Spirit is moving in our midst, calling us to refocus on the mission of the church as we face the challenges of this incredible post-Christendom world in which we live.

We have learned the hard way that instruction about the Bible and the Christian faith does not guarantee an experience of God's grace or a commitment to Christian discipleship. We have learned the hard way that gathering a group of individual children, youth, or adults in the same room does not guarantee Christian community. Nor does it guarantee effective teaching and learning. Yet we keep working to improve our Sunday schools as if the problem were with us and not with the system. As the new era continues to emerge, we must build new systems to meet contemporary needs and focus on the eternal mission of the church. These new systems may include Sunday school, but, more than likely, they will not be limited to traditional Sunday morning classes. It is only through a clear understanding of the mission of the church that we can build effective systems for teaching and learning.

## THE CHURCH'S MISSION TODAY

The mission of the church is to joyfully proclaim the good news of God's grace and to eagerly seek the fulfillment of God's reign in the world. It is to live as disciples of Jesus Christ so that our relationships and our world are transformed by God's Spirit. A disciple is one who follows a teacher. In the Christian community, that teacher is Jesus. Christian disciples seek to follow the example of Jesus in the way that they relate to God, to other human beings, and to the natural world.

Self-giving love characterized Jesus' life and ministry. A congregation centered in the gospel will take seriously its role as servant of the world. A congregation that focuses on the proclamation of the good news that God was in Christ reconciling the world to God's self will identify with and respond to the deep pain and brokenness of the world.

If this mission were to be described as an ongoing process in the life of the congregation, it might be described as follows:

- seeking and welcoming people into the body of Christ
- helping people to commit their lives to God
- nurturing people in faith
- sending people into the world to live lives of love and justice

This is not a linear process, but a circular or spiral one. Regardless of how long we have been a part of a congregation, we still need to be welcomed, we still need to experience God's grace, and we still need to strengthen our knowledge and skills for living as disciples. In addition, newcomers to a congregation may enter the process at any point. An invitation or welcome from a church member is not automatically the first step. Consider the following scenarios:

- Dana has not attended church since adolescence. Now a divorced mother of a two-year-old son, she is looking for safe, good quality childcare near her apartment. She notices that the United Methodist church in her neighborhood has a childcare center, and she remembers long-ago friends from Sunday school, camp, and vacation Bible school.
- Brad's family has just moved to a new city. It's been hard for Brad to get to know many of the members of his tenth grade classes. His new high school is so big and everyone is so busy! Brad thinks he might try out the youth group at the church down the street. Maybe some of his classmates go to church there.
- Sherrie and Dave are concerned about the growing number of homeless families in their city. They spend the first Thursday evening of every month working at a shelter, which includes a thrift store and job referral services. They're impressed that many of the volunteers they have met are from a local congregation.
- Rachel is a paralegal in a law firm. She and her friends enjoy dancing, going to concerts, and taking trips to the beach. But lately she's been wondering exactly where her life is headed. She decides to attend worship at the church around the corner from her condo, just to check it out.

The point is that no matter how people come to the church, they need to be welcomed, nurtured, and challenged to respond to God's call to discipleship. While few would argue with the above process, it has not been easy to implement it. In many congregations, the process has been segmented and farmed out to various committees and task forces. Seeking and welcoming people has been identified with evangelism. Helping people commit their lives to God has become a function of worship services. Teaching and learning have been delegated to nurture and education committees. Responsibility for sending out people to live lovingly and justly has been given to a missions, outreach, or social concerns committee.

The truth of the matter is that everything the church does should fully address this process. That includes the teaching ministry of the church. Those engaged in teaching and learning must attend to seeking and welcoming new people into small groups. They must understand that their task is to help people get to know God and feel connected to God. In order to live each day as Christian disciples, they must create the learning environments that help people reflect on their experience in light of the Scriptures and Christian tradition.

Congregations must begin to pay attention to the processes through which they regularly engage people in learning to love God and serve God's people. I believe this takes place in the ebb and flow between the total congregation gathered for worship and congregational members participating in small groups for study, reflection, support, and practice.

Congregational leaders must spend time in prayer and Bible study that focuses on Christian discipleship. They must seek to discern God's vision for their congregation. And they must take the time necessary for developing small-group leadership that helps the entire congregation engage in lifelong learning and growing in faith.

At this point it may be helpful to clarify the relationship between mission and vision. Every Christian congregation has the same mission—to proclaim the good news of God's grace and move toward the fulfillment of God's kingdom. Every congregation must continually evaluate how they create a hospitable climate for encountering God through Jesus Christ and discovering what it means to follow Christ in daily life.

Yet each Christian congregation is unique because of the community in which it is found, because of the people who are a part of the congregation, and because of the specific needs and gifts represented within the congregation and community. Vision refers to the mental image of how God intends a particular congregation to live out its mission. The vision for a congregation of 65 people in rural

Iowa will look different than the vision of a congregation of 560 people in suburban New Jersey. And that congregation's vision will differ from the vision of a 250-member congregation in an inner-city area of California.

That is true because discipleship is formed within the context of a congregation's community, needs, concerns, gifts, and opportunities. Just as Jesus responded differently to each person he met, depending on his or her needs, congregations must build a shared vision for living out their mission depending on where they find themselves and who they are. When they do, their vision has the power to pull them into the future.

If teaching and learning continue to play a vital role in building a congregation's vision and supporting its mission, there must be significant shifts in how we teach and learn. (See the chart below.)

As you read the left column, consider whether or not this accurately describes current systems for teaching and learning in many congregations. What is missing from this column? What should be removed from the column? What should be revised?

## Contemporary Shifts in Teaching and Learning

| Moving From | Moving To |
| --- | --- |
| Programming/Schooling/Activity Model | Christian Formation Model |
| Training People | Learning Together |
| Teaching as Instruction/Information | Teaching for Transformation |
| Focusing on the Institution | Focusing on Living as God's People |
| One Size Fits All | Building Shared Vision Locally |
| Focusing on the Parts | Focusing on the Whole |

I suggest that, for the most part, our current structures and processes have supported a schooling model in which information is primary. The teacher, pastor, or education committee has responsibility for selecting what content will be taught, when classes are offered, and which curriculum resources are appropriate. Congregations have assumed that "programs" that have been successful in one congregation will be successful in their congregation.

If this schooling model was built on the assumption that people can learn all they need to know in childhood, as suggested earlier, then it is also assumed that adults no longer need to learn. For those congregations that do value adult Christian education, there may be no plan in place to help adults reflect on the meaning of Christian discipleship, evaluate their spiritual lives, and plan for learning and practice around their needs for spiritual growth. Few congregations have consistently developed basic, intermediate, and advanced opportunities for adult Christian formation.

In addition, few congregations have seriously considered the integration of Christian education, worship, evangelism, stewardship, and mission. The larger the congregation, the more complex this integration becomes. It has been far too easy for each group of laity and church staff to focus on their specific responsibilities, rather than on the "big picture." Even when the big picture is acknowledged and a particular committee's work is understood in relation to the mission and vision of the congregation, it is unusual for that to be true for every committee, or for the committee to take the time needed to build a system that does consistently relate its work to the whole.

Now read the right column in the chart on page 21. What images come to mind when you read this column? Do these suggested shifts accurately represent where you believe our congregations need to be heading? What is missing from this column? What would you revise or eliminate?

These suggested shifts are an attempt to describe systems for teaching and learning that will move our congregations toward focusing on their mission and vision, rather than on building a strong institution. If we believe that the gospel of Jesus Christ has the power to transform the world, then we must be serious and intentional about immersing our children, youth, and adults in that gospel.

As people come together to pray and study the Scriptures, they test their ideas of what it means to be a disciple in their particular place. They prepare for participation in worship and service. They reflect on the needs of the community, state, nation, and world, and they learn how the church is responding to those needs. They discover opportunities for addressing those needs directly.

Congregational leaders can use Sunday school classes, Bible study groups, other small-group ministries, and one-on-one relationships to listen and reflect on how their congregational members view the needs of the congregation and community. It is often in small groups or through relationships with a mentor that people discover their gifts for ministry. Effective teachers will be in touch with how people are expressing their interests and will help them articulate and claim their spiritual gifts, as well as practice using them.

## FIVE CRITICAL PROCESSES FOR TEACHING/LEADING

As our congregations clarify their understanding of the church's mission and their particular vision for ministry, they will determine what shifts need to be made to move their congregation toward their vision. They will be able to identify and develop leadership for the teaching ministry that supports their mission and vision.

While a congregation may recognize that they need leaders with specific skills and knowledge to address the issues facing their congregation, there are at least five critical processes that will help any teacher serve effectively in creating the climate for people to experience the kind of Christian community we have been talking about. These processes are

1. keeping in touch with God—how leaders can experience the presence of God through disciplined Christian habits, such as prayer and Bible study;

2. keeping in touch with God's people—how leaders can set aside their own agendas to listen to the deep yearnings of those in their small group or class;
3. keeping in touch with your experience—how leaders reflect on their experience in light of Scripture and the Christian tradition;
4. keeping in touch with the world—how leaders participate in the mission and ministry of the church;
5. keeping in touch with teaching—how leaders can create a climate that helps people experience the awe and mystery of God and build knowledge and skills for discipleship.

The remaining chapters of this book explore these critical processes. You will have already noted that these processes go beyond teaching methods and classroom instruction, which was the focus of the schooling model used during the Christendom Era. You also will have noted that my definition of a small group may include only two people. In the emerging era, congregations will need to provide a wide variety of mentoring/learning opportunities.

In addition to drawing on learnings from the Sunday school, I also have based these processes on the class meeting model of Christian formation and insights from contemporary business concepts of customer service. This is not as much an attempt to reclaim earlier models in discipleship or revitalize current systems of teaching and learning as it is an attempt to distill essential elements for effective leadership of small groups gathered for growth in faith and discipleship.

You are invited into a process of dialogue around these processes as you continue to clarify your own understanding of what it means to teach and learn for faithful discipleship. As you reflect on your reading, you probably will have other processes to add to the list. You may disagree with one or more of these processes. That's fine.

In times of radical change, we learn through experimentation. Don't worry about "right" answers. Instead, be open to God's Spirit as you explore the changing role of teaching for Christian formation. It's time to claim the promise of Jesus: "Those who abide in me [who are "in touch" with me] and I in them bear much fruit" (John 15:5). Happy abiding!

# GUIDE FOR GROUP USE

1. Read the biblical stories listed on page 9. Make a list of Jesus' characteristics related to how he responded to each person he encountered. Discuss how these characteristics relate to teaching and learning within the congregation.

2. Study Scripture passages that focus on discipleship. (You may want to use Luke 4:16-21; Matthew 25:31-46; Luke 10:25-42; Romans 12:1-21.) Identify behaviors, attitudes, values, and beliefs of a disciple, as described in these passages. Discuss how your system of teaching and learning supports discipleship. Name areas in which you need to improve.

3. Discuss the metaphor of *keeping in touch* as it relates to teaching and learning. What other metaphors and images represent this ministry for you? How can you effectively use these metaphors in building a congregational vision for teaching and learning?

4. Review the three eras of church history, as described by Loren Mead. What changes have you seen as the church has moved from the Christendom Era to the post-Christendom Era? What are the implications of these changes for teaching and learning?

# chapter 2

# Keeping in Touch With God

*Be still, and know that I am God!*

*Psalm 46:10*

I f we, as teachers and leaders, are to begin making the shifts in teaching and learning identified in Chapter 1, we must continually seek to know God. Otherwise, any changes we make will be grounded in our own opinions, rather than in God's will. (Even if you disagree with the shifts suggested in the previous chapter and are satisfied with your congregation's teaching ministry, you still must continually seek to know God. Otherwise, the structures and programs you institute may be focused on your own will or desire.) It is only through knowing God that we can begin to discern in what direction God's Spirit is leading us.

This knowledge of God is a gift. It comes not from our own efforts, but through learning to be attentive to God's Spirit. In *Making All Things New: An Invitation to the Spiritual Life* (© 1981 Henri J. M. Nouwen; published by HarperCollins Publishers, Inc.; page 65), Henri J. M. Nouwen writes:

The Holy Spirit…lifts us up into the kingdom of God's love. But to say that being lifted up into the kingdom of love is a divine gift does not mean that we wait passively until the gift is offered to us. Jesus tells us to set our hearts on the kingdom. Setting our hearts on something involves not only serious aspiration but also strong determination. A spiritual life requires human effort.

So how are we to "set our hearts on the kingdom"? Throughout the centuries Christians have discovered a variety of methods that have kept them in touch with God. These methods have been called spiritual disciplines, holy habits, or means of grace. Spiritual disciplines are practices that assist us in offering ourselves to God and receiving God's grace. They help us create the space we need to listen to God, speak to God, and understand ourselves in relation to God and one another through Jesus Christ.

As we practice the spiritual disciplines, we discover the innate rhythm of the spiritual life. As we grow in God's grace, we learn to balance working and resting, speaking and listening, being and doing. This rhythm is rather like a dance of engagement and response, with God as our partner.

The essence of this rhythm is corporate, as well as individual. God has called us into covenant community with God and with one another. True Christian discipleship is not a private, individualized matter. Rather, Christian discipleship occurs within the framework of God's people and God's world.

Spiritual disciplines strengthen our connection to all God's people and help us understand the context for serving God throughout the world. As we consistently exercise these means of grace, we find the patterns of daily, weekly, monthly, and yearly practices that sustain our spirits, keep us focused on God, and transform us into the people and communities God intends us to be.

## THE MEANS OF GRACE

John Wesley understood the means of grace to include
- prayer
- studying the Scriptures

- worship (especially the Lord's Supper)
- fasting
- Christian "conferencing"
- acts of mercy

Through these spiritual practices we discover what it means to fully love God and love God's people. If a congregation intends this to happen through its teaching and learning, then it is essential that teachers, small-group leaders, and other mentors must be consistently developing their own spiritual lives. Only as we pay attention to God at work in our lives can we create the space for others to notice and respond to God at work in their lives.

If, then, it is vitally important for teachers to use the means of grace, let us further explore these various disciplines. But before we begin our exploration, a word of caution: These practices, to be means of *grace*, are not governed by a rigid set of rules that must be rigorously followed in order for the practices to be effective. What we are striving for is an attitude of openness and receptivity to God's presence. Such an attitude leads to trust, joy, and hope.

## Prayer

Any reading of the Christian classics puts prayer front and center in the spiritual life. Our mothers and fathers in the faith learned from experience that prayer was the key to maintaining their relationship with God. And so it is with us.

There are many ways to pray. Teachers may find some of the following methods helpful in developing their prayer life:

- using written prayers found in devotional materials or books
- meditating on Scripture, especially the Psalms
- using a "breath" prayer (repeating a phrase as you inhale and repeating another as you exhale; for example, "Jesus, be my guide [inhale], and I will follow you [exhale]")
- spontaneous prayer
- silence

While these methods may be familiar to you already, I will have to admit that they weren't always familiar to me. As I continue to develop my prayer life, one of my great joys is discovering new methods of prayer that open my eyes and ears to God in ways that I haven't yet experienced.

As a person who processes information through speaking, one of my greatest learnings has been around the need for silence and listening as a part of prayer. I am learning the wisdom of Psalm 46:10: "Be still, and know that I am God!" In order for me to keep in touch with God, I have had to develop the skill of being still, of focusing, of centering all my thoughts on God.

When I worked in the local church, I would be so busy and focused on my role as a church staff member that I rarely planned time for prayer and meditation as part of my schedule. In fact, I didn't understand that spending time in prayer was a part of my role as church staff.

When I joined the staff of a general church agency, I continued to be distracted by meetings, preparations for workshops, correspondence, telephone calls, and so forth. I rarely stopped long enough to spend any focused time in prayer or any other means of grace. The demands of my job soon taught me the folly of this oversight. I had to come to a point of sheer desperation before the discipline of prayer became vitally important to me.

In 1994 I was assigned to the design team for Youth '95, a national youth ministry conference that involved 4,000 youth and their adult leaders. Although I begged and pleaded to be on another committee, I was asked to serve on the team that planned worship and Bible study for the event. After nearly twenty years as a professional Christian educator, I was acutely aware of my limitations in youth ministry and harbored no delusions regarding my effectiveness on this team.

When it became evident that my begging and pleading was not going to get me anywhere, I realized I would indeed have to help plan Bible study and worship for 4,000 adolescents. There was only one thing left to do: throw myself on God's mercy! And that's exactly what I did.

I reminded God on a regular basis that I was not capable of the task before me. I claimed with all my heart God's promise to be with me. I trusted in God's love, not only for me and the other members of the planning team, but also for all those young people who were making their plans to be in Salt Lake City in July 1995. And I claimed, with the apostle Paul, that in my weakness is God's strength, in my inability is God's ability, in my limitation is God's opportunity.

I began to pray every day for the design team and the participants of Youth '95. And when those prayers began to see fruit, I added my coworkers, neighbors, family members, and friends from church. When those prayers engaged my heart and mind with the heart and mind of Christ, I added the mayor, governor, President, and members of Congress.

What I began to learn is that prayer is the foundation for shaping my day in God's love and light. Through prayer we are reminded of who God is, who we are as God's children, and how God continually is present for us. Prayer is the vehicle for aligning our wills to God's will, for laying before God all our wants and needs, opportunities and struggles, and asking for wisdom in sorting out what we really need.

As you pray, consider beginning with silence to prepare yourself to be in God's presence. Although there is no predetermined order to follow in prayer, you may naturally move from silence into thanksgiving. In corporate worship our prayers of thanksgiving are general. However, in personal prayer we can thank God for specific blessings, such as this experience of friendship, today's beauty, this experience of healing.

Prayer should also include confession. We need to be realistic about ourselves and honest with ourselves and with God. Confession keeps us from hiding from God. If we fail to confess, we can pretend that God isn't noticing us. And we can pretend that our lives are in good shape and "all's right with the world." When we open up the lines of communication with God and acknowledge the truth, we find freedom and release from anxiety, stress, and alienation. Confession enables us to recognize and accept God's pardon.

Praying for others also should be a focus of our spiritual lives. Intercessory prayer has been described as cooperation with God. As we intercede for specific people, we bear one another's burdens. As we lift up the needs of another human being and wait in silence, we may be prompted by God's Spirit to some action.

Some of those specific people for us, as teachers, will be our group members. As we lay before God the needs and concerns of our group, we can begin to see our group members through God's eyes. We can discern how God wants to build us into a Christian community. We can receive guidance for planning and learning that intersects with and responds to our class members' needs.

Prayer also includes petition. We pray for our own needs after thanking God for God's good gifts, confessing our faults and receiving God's pardon, and praying for others. This is not a prayer of selfishness, but a prayer for grace. It is a prayer for help in "setting our hearts on the kingdom." In Matthew 11:28-30 we read: "Come to me, all you that are weary and are carrying heavy burdens, and I will give you rest. Take my yoke upon you, and learn from me... My yoke is easy, and my burden is light." Through petition, God shares our burdens and sustains us for responsible discipleship in the world.

## Studying the Scriptures

As with all the means of grace, the primary purpose of studying the Bible is to encounter the transforming presence of God. As we read the stories of how God's people have understood God throughout the ages, we begin to connect our stories with theirs. We connect our stories with God's story.

In order for this to happen, we must be consistent and systematic about our study. It is when we become thoroughly familiar with the Scriptures that we are able to hear God speaking to us. With this as our goal, information about the Scriptures leads to transformation.

For Wesley, this meant reading the Bible every day—morning and evening. During the course of a year he read through the Old Testament at least once and the New Testament several times. To guide his reading, he used the *Book of Common Prayer*. Through his reading he sought to know God's will, to be open to the Holy Spirit, and to put into practice what he was learning.

For me this is certainly a worthy goal for teachers and small-group leaders today. The Bible itself speaks to the importance of study in relation to transformation. In Romans 12:2 we read: "Do not be conformed to this world, but be transformed by the renewing of your minds, so that you may discern what is the will of God—what is good and acceptable and perfect."

To study effectively, Richard J. Foster suggests the following four steps (*Celebration of Discipline: The Path to Spiritual Growth*; HarperCollins Publishers, Inc., 1988). First, he believes that our study should include repetition. Repetition serves to develop habits of thought, which can lead to changed behavior. Repetition is also foundational in building corporate memory—remembering what God has done and how people of faith have responded to God's initiative. Teachers who are immersed in the Scripture play an active role in providing a link for their group members to that corporate memory.

Second, Foster reminds us to concentrate. Concentration focuses our attention and keeps us centered on what we are studying. Concentration increases our ability to retain and retrieve information in a way that continues to shape us into the image of Christ.

Foster's third step in studying the Scriptures is comprehension. What did the writer say? What did the writer mean? What were the circumstances being addressed in the writing? As we develop our understanding of what we are studying, we are better able to evaluate what we read and apply it to our own situation.

Teachers will find it helpful to use a variety of study resources as they strive for comprehension of Scripture. These resources may include a Bible atlas, Bible concordance, Bible dictionary, and Bible commentaries. At times it is beneficial to read a Scripture passage in several translations in order to explore the passage in depth.

Foster's fourth and last step for study is reflection. He defines *reflection* as recognizing the significance of what we are studying. Reflection assists us in seeing things from God's perspective. It leads to insight and provides us with the ability to see our reality and judge it in light of God's Word. As we reflect on Scripture, we listen for God's voice and allow ourselves to be addressed by God.

The kind of study described above should lead to and enhance our devotional reading of Scripture, which is essentially formational. As we discover the meaning of the biblical texts themselves, we perceive how the text relates to us and how we live in relation to others and the world.

For centuries, Christians have used a method called *lectio divina* (divine or sacred reading) in their devotional reading of Scripture. The four steps of this method are

1. *Lectio*—This refers to reading the text. During this step, one focuses on what the Scripture passage says. Some people find it helpful to imagine themselves in the story. Who is there? What is happening? How do those present respond to what is happening?

2. *Meditatio*—This, not surprisingly, involves meditation. As we meditate on the text, we get in touch with how we are feeling and what we are thinking. Meditation engages the heart as well as the mind. Through meditation we make connections between our experience and the meaning unfolding through the Scripture.

3. *Oratio*—This is associated with spoken words, particularly prayer. This is prayer that emerges from our meditation. When we are confronted with what God has to say to us and with what God is doing in our lives, we are acutely aware of the pain and struggle involved in faithful discipleship. Our prayer becomes confession and repentance.

   When we suddenly hear a word of grace spoken to our deepest wounds, or otherwise recognize the wonder of God's creative presence, we respond in praise and thanksgiving. When we identify within the biblical story an image or situation that relates to someone in our family, community, or world, we offer intercessory prayer on their behalf and pray for God's direction in how we respond.

4. *Contemplatio*—This refers to the quiet rest of contemplation and silence. As we come to the close of our devotional reading, we clear our minds and attempt simply to "be." It is the opportunity to let go of all expectations except to be in God's presence. Contemplation involves waiting, openness, and receptivity.

Teachers who regularly study the Bible and read it devotionally have enormous opportunity to introduce the living Word to their group members. As they share their love of the Scriptures with children, youth, and adults, they help foster that same love in those with whom they teach and learn.

## Worship

Participation in worship is essential in the spiritual formation of teachers and small-group leaders because corporate worship grounds us within the Christian community. Worship sets the context for all our activity, including teaching and learning.

Through baptism we affirm that God has taken the initiative to seek us and make covenant with us. We are welcomed into the Christian community, and we promise to support one another in growing in faith and discipleship.

Around the Lord's Table we remember Jesus and celebrate his continuing presence with us. We identify with that band of twelve who gathered with Jesus at his last meal, and we anticipate being united with Christ at the heavenly banquet.

In worship the gospel is proclaimed, and we are asked to respond. In worship we claim our identity as the body of Christ, and we acknowledge our need for one another. Once again we find the connection between our relationship with God and our relationship with other human beings. In worship these connections become grace-filled.

In the midst of the gathered community, we experience the presence of the risen Christ. Together we retell the stories of our faith and respond to the love, mercy, and grace of God.

Our worship serves as a testimony to who God is and what God has done (and is doing). In song, Scripture, sacrament, and prayer, we affirm the faith that sustains and guides us. Each time we gather, the Word is again made flesh and dwells among us. We join the "great...cloud of witnesses" (Hebrews 12:1) in testifying to God, whose grace and truth come to us through Jesus Christ.

Worship is also a sign of the covenant community God continues to create. God's promise to be our God and our promise to be God's people are at the heart of our Judeo-Christian heritage. We have been created for relationship, and this is nowhere more evident than in corporate worship. As we rehearse our faith, we strengthen our identity as God's people and build a shared vision of who God is calling us to be.

God's call to service in the name of Jesus is also an integral part of worship. The culminating act of the worship service, the sending forth, sends us out to live in the world as disciples of Jesus Christ. If we are indeed centered in God through Christ, then our worship must lead us to lives that mirror the example of Christ. Having been renewed in worship, we go out to live as "ambassadors for Christ," agents of reconciliation and hope (2 Corinthians 5:17-21).

## Fasting

Prior to the beginning of Jesus' public ministry, he spent forty days and forty nights in the wilderness. During this period in which he sought God's guidance in the shaping of his ministry, he fasted (Matthew 4:1-11; Luke 4:1-13).

This story from Jesus' own life illustrates the various purposes for fasting as a means of grace. First of all, as with all avenues of experiencing God's grace, fasting focuses attention on God. Fasting is not a matter of superior will power and self-control on our part, but rather serves as an acknowledgment of our dependence on God.

In the description of Jesus' temptation in the wilderness, we read that Satan encouraged Jesus to turn stones into bread as a way to satisfy his hunger. Jesus responded: "It is written, 'One does not live by bread alone, but by every word that comes from the mouth of God'" (Matthew 4:4). At this critical juncture in Jesus' life, he refused to turn to any source other than God for satisfying his needs—physical or spiritual.

Marjorie J. Thompson, reflecting on the purpose of fasting, asks:

Are we aware of how much sustains our life apart from physical food? Do we have an inner conviction that Christ is our life? We will comprehend little of how we are nourished by Christ until we have emptied ourselves of the kinds of sustenance that keep us content to live at life's surface (*Soul Feast: An Invitation to the Christian Spiritual Life*; © 1995 Marjorie J. Thompson; published by Westminster John Knox Press; page 71).

Thompson's questions are instructive because they remind us of our tendency to substitute other things for God. For some it may be food; for others it may be recognition, money, beauty, power. Any time we put our hopes and trust in something or someone other than God, we are in danger of sliding into idolatry.

Fasting may not, then, always be abstaining from food. We may find that we need to fast from excessive television viewing, from gossip, from spending money on clothing we don't need. What is it that you would substitute for God if you could? How is God calling you to fast?

We have the opportunity to begin answering these questions for ourselves as we combine fasting with prayer. This was the custom of Jesus, Moses, David, Elijah, and other saints throughout the ages. Fasting and prayer work together to empty the self, in order to be filled with God.

Prayer, as already described above, often includes confession and repentance. This humility of spirit opens us to the healing, restoring grace of God. In the Sermon on the Mount Jesus taught: "Blessed are those who hunger and thirst for righteousness, for they will be filled" (Matthew 5:6). In our fasting, as we focus on God through prayer, we claim Christ's promise to be filled.

Fasting, then, is in essence a tangible act of reverence for our God, who is Creator, Redeemer, and Sustainer. As teachers, when we center our attention on God and humbly ask for God's Spirit to guide us through fasting, we are taking advantage of yet one more means of experiencing the boundless grace of God. As we are nourished by the power of the Spirit, we are empowered to nourish others. In our teaching and leading, we become bread for the world.

## Christian Conferencing

The term *conferencing* may not be familiar to us, but the concept is. Christian conferencing refers to the community gathered for encouragement, support, fellowship, nurture, study, and service. In today's church, small-group ministries provide opportunities for us to conference with one another. Our Sunday school classes and other study groups should assist us in this effort. Finding ways to encourage Christian conferencing is an important consideration for those who lead small groups or Sunday school classes.

In Wesley's day, Christian conferencing took place through three specific structures: the societies, class meetings, and bands. These particular small groups will be described in Chapter 5. Here I want to point out two of their features related to this chapter. First, they were organized to support people in developing the disciplined spiritual life. Second, they fostered mutual accountability.

Each of these elements is important for our congregations today if we are to shift from a schooling model to a Christian formation model and from teaching for information to teaching for transformation. Why should we, as Christians, gather in small groups? Because we need each other.

It is not an easy thing to develop consistent patterns of prayer, Bible study, fasting, and the practice of acts of mercy. In a supportive group we can find practical help, as well as encouragement to keep trying. With those who also are seeking to follow Christ, we find the support we need to regularly assess our spiritual life and find direction for deepening our relationship with God.

There is another dimension to these group experiences. Spiritual discernment is often God's gift to God's people. Jesus promised his disciples: "For where two or three are gathered in my name, I am there among them" (Matthew 18:20). God in Christ comes to us in the experience of Christian community. Together we test our concepts of God and of Christian discipleship. We reflect on our daily practice of devotion and service. We are led by God's Spirit into new avenues of God's grace.

In *Life Together*, Dietrich Bonhoeffer writes:

> God has put this Word into the mouth of [others] in order that it may be communicated to [us]. When one person is struck by the Word, he speaks it to others.... Therefore, the Christian needs another Christian who speaks God's Word to him (© 1954 HarperCollins Publishers, Inc.; pages 22–23).

Bonhoeffer goes on to say that in Christian community we learn to live together. Through Christ whatever has potential for dividing us is abolished. We become brothers and sisters for one another and understand ourselves as forever connected to God, humanity, and all creation through Jesus Christ.

With whom do our teachers and small-group leaders conference? Where do they turn for support and encouragement, thereby experiencing God's grace? How does the concept of Christian conferencing affect our planning of teachers' meetings? These are important questions for those with responsibility for supporting the spiritual formation of teachers and other group leaders.

## Acts of Mercy

Our connection to all humanity is the foundation for living mercifully and justly. This dynamic relationship between loving God and loving neighbor is at the heart of Wesley's understanding of Christian spirituality.

As always, that understanding has its basis in Scripture. Consider the following passages:

- Matthew 25:31-46—parable of the Great Judgment
- Mark 12:28-34—the Great Commandment
- Luke 10:25-37—parable of the good Samaritan
- John 21:15-17—Jesus' command to Peter to feed his sheep

These passages are only a few of the instances in which Jesus taught his disciples to live out their love of God through service to others. However, Jesus not only taught about service but also exemplified it. He fed the hungry, cured the sick, and befriended the friendless. The gospel accounts of Jesus' ministry are a vivid testimony that the words and deeds of Jesus were good news to the poor and disenfranchised.

Richard J. Foster helps us understand how the discipline of service becomes a means of experiencing God's grace. He distinguishes between choosing to serve and choosing to be a servant. He writes:

> When we choose to serve we are still in charge. We decide whom we will serve and when we will serve.... But when we choose to be a servant we give up the right to be in charge.... We become available and vulnerable (*Celebration of Discipline: The Path to Spiritual Growth*; © 1988 Richard J. Foster; published by HarperCollins Publishers, Inc.; page 115).

The grace of God comes to us again and again when we surrender our excessive need to be in control and claim our reliance on God. Through servanthood we practice hospitality to others because we have first experienced God's hospitality toward us.

As hospitable servants in Christ, we respond to the needs of the world. We do not offer our service to those who meet our criteria, whatever that may be. Rather, we follow the example of our crucified Lord, pouring out ourselves for the sake of others. This servanthood leads, not to a sense of duty, but to an expression of love.

For teachers it may be tempting to assume that teaching is their service to others. In light of the multiple demands on our time and energy, it may even be greatly desired. And certainly, teaching is a wonderful gift to our congregations.

However, as the body of Christ, we must continue to hear God's call to service beyond the four walls of the church building. As teachers, small-group leaders, and other mentors continue to strengthen their relationship with God, they will discover ways in which they live out their faith at home, at work, and at leisure, as well as through their participation in congregational life.

# GUIDE FOR GROUP USE

1. After reading this chapter, discuss your understanding of how the spiritual practices of prayer, Bible study, worship, fasting, Christian conferencing, and acts of mercy can be means of God's grace. You may want to discuss personal experiences related to these practices.

2. Review the opportunities your congregation offered for teacher development during the past twelve to eighteen months. In what ways did the congregation specifically provide support and encouragement for the development of a disciplined spiritual life?

3. Brainstorm a list of possibilities for strengthening the prayer life of your teachers and small-group leaders. Include several teachers and group leaders in this exercise. Formulate a plan to be tested with the rest of your teachers.

4. Consider how your teacher/leader development opportunities might become experiences of Christian conferencing. Discuss what you would need to do in order for that to become reality.

5. Many congregations currently schedule Sunday school and worship at the same time. This may mean that teachers are unable to attend worship. Reflect on worship as a means of grace and the implications of creating a schedule that eliminates the possibility of teachers' participation in worship.

**chapter 3**

# KEEPING IN TOUCH WITH GOD'S PEOPLE

*Beloved, let us love one another, because love is from God; everyone who loves is born of God and knows God.*

*I John 4:7*

I n *Life Together,* Dietrich Bonhoeffer writes:

> Christianity means community through Jesus Christ and in Jesus Christ. No Christian community is more or less than this. Whether it be a brief, single encounter or the daily fellowship of years, Christian community is only this. We belong to one another only through and in Jesus Christ (© 1954 HarperCollins Publishers, Inc.; page 21).

What a powerful statement! It is possible, and certainly desirable, to experience this statement as truth in and through the small-group experiences provided by our congregations. These experiences, guided by a skilled leader, have the potential of shaping our understanding of ourselves as part of the body of Christ.

Teachers who are interested in building strong, healthy relationships with and among their group members will, therefore, do all in their power to be in touch with their group members. This entails more than a superficial knowledge of the people in their care. It involves a commitment to maintaining long-term, ever-deepening relationships with those they teach.

This in-depth knowledge not only builds a sense of belonging but also shapes the learning environment itself. Remember the shift from training people to learning together identified in Chapter 1? This shift can happen only when group members become active contributors to the teaching/learning process, rather than passive recipients.

It may be somewhat of an overstatement to say that in the schooling model, class members are seen as objects, rather than as subjects. However, I would suggest that is not far off the mark at times. As long as our congregations shape learning experiences with the assumption that the teacher is an expert of content knowledge, which other people should know whether they have asked for the information or not, we are in danger of objectifying the people we seek to draw into community.

If we are striving to create sacred space in which people relate to one another and to God through Jesus Christ, then we will need to identify and articulate the models for teaching and learning that most effectively allow this to emerge. We will shape our teaching and learning to allow people, individually and corporately, to discover who God is calling them to be.

This most likely means that we will have to experiment with creating new models. In this time of rapid change, we often know more about what doesn't work than about what does. Learning from failures, as well as from successes, is a key characteristic for growing spiritually. Learning from our failures can also help us improve the way in which we shape our learning environments.

Small-group leaders who hope to participate in creating new models for Christian formation appropriate to today's world need to develop an attitude of partnership with those whom they teach and lead. It is through keeping in touch with God's people that the entire community of faith is blessed.

# IN TOUCH WITH DIVERSITY

One of the ways we keep in touch with people is by recognizing and seeking to understand the diversity among the people in our small groups. There are obvious differences among people, such as age, gender, and racial background. Each of these differences creates significant variations in the way individuals perceive situations and make judgments about what others say and do. Our personal histories are always present in any learning environment. Those histories will have an impact on how we choose to participate within the group.

In addition, there are other differences between people that may not be quite as obvious. However, when we begin to pay attention, we will discover that the people in our small group differ in how they learn and in the way they experience God. In part, these differences are a function of a person's personality.

## Personality Types

The mother-daughter team of Katharine Cook Briggs and Isabel Briggs Myers worked together for many years to develop a tool for understanding personality. This survey instrument is called the Myers-Briggs Type Indicator® personality inventory. The two women based much of their work on the theories of psychologist Carl Jung.

The Myers-Briggs Type Indicator® looks at four sets of preferences on a continuum:
- extraversion/introversion
- sensing/intuition
- thinking/feeling
- judging/perceiving

Depending on the circumstances, a person may demonstrate a variety of behaviors representing the above pairs. However, type theory suggests that each person, over time, will show a preference for one or the other in each pair. These preferences are a part of what makes each of us a unique individual.

## EXTRAVERSION AND INTROVERSION

Let's take a look at the first pair of preferences, extraversion and introversion. We are familiar with these terms. Generally, we use words such as *outgoing, vivacious,* and *friendly* to categorize an extravert. We may use words such as *shy, reserved,* and *quiet* to describe introverts.

Actually, this pair of preferences has little to do with friendliness. Extraverts and introverts can be friendly. The difference is in how they are energized. Extraverts find being with people energizing. They draw energy from the outer world of people and things. Introverts draw on the inner world of ideas for energy and sustenance. Extraverts enjoy a crowd and have a wide variety of acquaintances. Introverts prefer staying in contact with a few, close friends.

One of the obvious ways this pair of preferences can impact a group setting relates to communication patterns. Extraverts are quick to speak, and they process information verbally. Since they may be prone to "thinking out loud," they can monopolize the conversation. Introverts process information internally and usually think about what they are going to say before they say it.

Teachers and small-group leaders should vary group activities to accommodate these preferences. Opportunities to journal, to pray silently, and to write down thoughts prior to speaking are all ways to give introverts the space they need to participate. Dividing the group into smaller groups can appeal to extraverts and introverts alike. An introverted group member will feel more comfortable speaking with a few people, and an extraverted group member won't have to curb his or her desire to talk as much.

Many leaders have discovered that one-on-one relationships are beneficial for supporting the spiritual growth of people. Mentors, or spiritual friends, have opportunities to develop long-term relationships with people that can make significant contributions to their faith formation. A mentoring relationship can be of great benefit to extraverts and introverts alike. Extraverts profit from having someone with whom they can talk about faith issues. More introverted individuals may enjoy working with a mentor because they find it more enjoyable to interact with one person at a time. A relationship with a respected friend can significantly shape group members' understanding of who they are in relationship to God. They can address life issues in a safe place with a trusted companion and benefit from relating to another person who will share their struggles, joys, and questions.

## SENSING AND INTUITION

This set of preferences relates to the ways in which people take in and use information. Those who prefer sensing gather information through their five senses—hearing, sight, smell, touch, taste. They tend to be practical, realistic, and factual. They are frequently described as down-to-earth, no-nonsense people. They often appreciate tradition and want to know that activities in which they participate will serve a useful purpose. They have a good grasp of details, facts, and order.

People who prefer intuition gather information in a less concrete way. Intuitive people depend on their hunches. They enjoy considering how things can be improved and are future-oriented. They enjoy learning new skills and may grow bored with routine. They will focus more on the meaning of an activity and less on the details.

In a group setting, the difference between those who are more intuitive and those who are more sensing often displays itself in obvious ways. While intuitives are discussing the cosmic significance of the Christ Event, the sensors want to know who will be in charge of publicity for the class retreat coming up next month. The two types speak different languages and look at the world in such diverse ways that they may find it difficult to understand the others' priorities.

Group leaders who are aware of the gifts that intuitives and sensors bring to any setting will be able to plan group activities with those gifts in mind. Conversations relating faith to daily life should be practical as well as theoretical. Intuitives will enjoy discussing who are our neighbors; sensors will need to see direct implications for how they live as husbands and wives, employees, and friends.

Sensors may enjoy using Bible atlases, concordances, and other study tools. They will respond to details about Bible times, the life of Jesus, the books of the Bible, and so forth. Intuitives will enjoy discussing theology and the meaning of the passages they are studying.

### THINKING AND FEELING

The way people make decisions is also related to personality types. People who are feeling types tend to make decisions based on values and relationships. People who are thinking types tend to use logic and data to make decisions.

Those who prefer thinking are often characterized as analytical, objective, and concerned with the principles of justice and fairness. People who prefer feeling are often described as tactful, empathetic, and seekers of harmony. If we are not careful, we may label thinkers with words such as *unfeeling, cold,* or *distant*. Likewise, we may consider feelers to be *erratic, over-emotional,* or *illogical*. Feelers and thinkers both have emotions; however, they express their emotions differently.

Small groups in the church will include feelers and thinkers. Effective group leadership will help feelers articulate what they think about faith issues. Leaders will also assist thinkers in acknowledging their feelings.

### JUDGING AND PERCEIVING

The last set of preferences relates to judging and perceiving. Judging types appreciate order, structure, and planning ahead. Perceiving types generally assume there is additional information that may be forthcoming at any moment; therefore, they tend to avoid coming to closure.

Perceiving types are more than willing to take things as they come and tend to be informal and less comfortable in institutional settings. Judging types like to know what to expect. They understand routine and are good at meeting deadlines and completing organizational tasks.

In a group setting, people who prefer an open-ended approach will bring spontaneity and freshness to the group life. People who prefer routine and order will keep the group grounded and on task. Each type, as the others above, brings a variety of gifts to a group. We only have to open our minds and hearts in order to receive their gifts.

The previous descriptions of the four pairs of preferences are brief out of necessity. The four pairs combine to create sixteen different combinations or types. The bibliography at the back of this book lists several good resources that will help you understand personality type theory more fully.

## Spiritual Types

Urban T. Holmes, in his book *A History of Christian Spirituality: An Analytical Introduction* (HarperCollins, 1981), seeks to describe patterns of Christian spirituality. He suggests that people tend primarily to access "knowledge" of God through logic and reason or through feelings and intuition. He also believes that as we seek this knowledge, our perception of God may be direct or indirect.

While we may use different approaches at any given time, we tend to have a preference. Some people generally use their thoughts to appropriate information about God, while others use their feelings. Some generally perceive God to be immanent, involved in the details of our lives, ever ready to come to our assistance. Other people usually perceive that God is ultimately unknowable, transcendent, mysterious, and awesome.

Holmes hypothesizes four spiritual types based on combinations of the above representations. People who are Type 1 (my designation, not Holmes') understand God primarily through their thoughts and believe that God is present in their daily lives. Type 1 people enjoy discussing theology and study. They express their faith through what they think about God. They are interested in discerning the will of God and seeing God's active presence in the world. For Type 1 people, content is primary. They are most interested in fulfilling their vocation in life.

People who are Type 2 also believe that God is present in our daily lives. However, they generally understand God through their feelings. It is important for them to be in relationship with God and with others in the congregation. They express feelings easily and enjoy praying aloud, singing, and witnessing to their faith. Their focus is on transformation and personal renewal. Their agenda is achieving holiness of life.

People who are Type 3 also make use of their feelings in understanding God; however, they perceive God as transcendent. Type 3's are introspective, reflective, and enjoy silence and contemplation. They find fulfillment in the "journey" toward God. Christian mystics are an example of Type 3. They seek renewal of the inner life.

Type 4 people understand God as mysterious and transcendent. But they have moved to the thinking mode in receiving and assimilating information about God. Their focus is on the ideal, as represented by the kingdom of God. Their agenda is the transformation of society; therefore, they tend to equate prayer and theology with action. This type is the least likely to participate in congregational life. They prefer to be living out their faith in the world.

Corinne Ware—the Associate Director of the Master of Arts in Pastoral Ministry degree at the Episcopal Seminary of the Southwest in Austin, Texas—has developed a survey based on Holmes' work to help identify people's ways of experiencing God. Her book, *Discover Your Spiritual Type: A Guide to Individual and Congregational Growth* (The Alban Institute, 1995), is easy to read and includes the survey instrument as well as more information about each of the above spiritual types.

According to Ware, while each of us has a preference for one type, we should seek a balanced spiritual life. She suggests that the spiritual type opposite ours is the type from which we can learn the most. (For Type 1's, the opposite is Type 3. Type 4 and Type 2 are opposites.) She encourages us to reflect on the strengths of the spiritual type that is opposite ours in order to discern what God may be calling us to learn.

Ware suggests that the spiritual types closest to us may be the ones that annoy us the most. If we're not careful, we can fall into the trap of judging the way in which other people express their faith, especially if they don't express their faith in the same ways we do.

Type 1's, with their emphasis on content, can be categorized as impersonal, formal, and disengaged. Type 2's will be criticized as being pietistic and sentimental. Type 3's will be judged as living in "an alternate reality." Type 4's can be criticized for their zealousness that borders on tunnel vision.

Teachers and small-group leaders can help their group members understand and appreciate the different ways in which people understand God. When we have information that illuminates the behavior of others around us, we are less likely to draw inaccurate conclusions about their faith and their relationship with God.

Teachers and leaders who recognize the spiritual types represented in their group will also build on the strengths of these types. They will pay attention to the way in which they lead learning experiences, group-building activities, and group worship.

For example, groups with several Type 4's should be sure to include opportunities for service outside the classroom, such as working in a homeless shelter or building a house through Habitat for Humanity. If you have several Type 3's in your group, you may want to suggest journaling. For Type 2's, be sure to include plenty of opportunities for interacting with other group members. If you have Type 1's in your group, provide study experiences that include content and reflection.

## IN TOUCH THROUGH LISTENING

How will we discover what kind of personality types our class members have? How will we understand what kinds of spiritual types are represented in our small groups? How will we plan our classes and group meetings to illuminate the life experiences of our group members? Simply put, we must listen.

I like to think of this kind of listening as listening without an agenda. This kind of listening is one in which we lay aside our desires, our assumptions, and our goals. We simply open ourselves to receive the gift of another human being. We open ourselves to their desires, their dreams, their pain, and their struggles.

There are several tools you can use to do this kind of listening. When you are initiating a conversation with one of your group members, you can use open-ended questions to encourage sharing. For example, if you are talking with an adult, you might ask any of the following kinds of questions:

- Tell me about being a member of this Sunday school class.
- Tell me about being a member of this congregation.
- Tell me about being a teacher (lawyer, secretary, and so forth).

If you are talking with a teenager, you might say:

- Tell me about being a member of this youth group.
- Tell me about being in the tenth grade.
- Tell me about being an only child.

If you are talking with a child, you might say:

- Tell me about your school.
- Tell me about worship in this congregation.
- Tell me about your family.

When asked an open-ended question, the person can decide what and how much he or she wants to tell you about whatever you are asking. As you listen, follow up the initial response with additional questions. You might say, "Tell me more" or "What else?"

You can also ask questions for clarification and understanding. As people talk, take notes to help you remember what is being said. As the conversation continues, you can probe for deeper understanding by saying something such as, "Earlier you said you were enjoying your new job. What is it that you enjoy about it?" or "When you said you don't consider yourself a good student, I wasn't sure what you meant. Can you say more about that?"

You will also want to listen for words that are repeated often. These words may represent significant meaning in the speaker's life. You can use those words to indicate your understanding of what is being said. You may also use those words to ask for further clarification.

You may want to have two or three additional questions ready to ask in case you need them. While my experience has been that the one open-ended question—such as, "Tell me about…"—will give you plenty to talk about, it never hurts to be prepared.

This kind of listening assists people in storytelling. Since identifying our own stories and how they connect to the biblical story is essential for spiritual growth, you are offering a great service to those in your class or small group when you invite them to tell their stories.

You will benefit from this kind of listening and dialogue in one-on-one conversations. It's possible to include some of the same kinds of questions in a group setting; however, if your goal is to become better acquainted with your group members, I suggest that you set up personal interviews with them throughout the course of the year.

This may seem awkward at first, but I encourage you to try it. I have found that people really like to talk. Of all the people I have interviewed, only one or two were reticent about sharing. And just so you will be prepared, count on about an hour's worth of conversation. Two to three questions answered in depth will take that long.

If one of your group members has initiated the conversation (or when you're listening in a group setting), you can paraphrase what you are hearing in order to check the accuracy of your understanding. Listen for the main idea being expressed. Take note of the nouns and verbs. Then restate the main idea in your own words. For example, you might begin with, "If I understand you correctly, you are saying…" Use paraphrasing whenever you want to be sure of the content of what is being said.

Since communication involves more than words, part of listening will be paying attention to the tone of voice and posture of the speaker. We have probably caught ourselves drumming our fingers on the table when we are impatient. When we are embarrassed, our faces may turn red. When we feel uncomfortable in a group, we may withdraw or become combative. Withdrawal and readiness for combat each has a set of behaviors that goes with it. When we withdraw, we may cross our arms across our chests and turn our heads away from the group. When we are feeling combative, we may lean forward, frown, and raise our voices.

Group leaders need to pay attention to these verbal and physical clues to the emotional state of our group members. We also need to keep in mind that the same set of behaviors may mean more than one thing. I like to laugh, and I do so often. I laugh in a wide variety of situations. When I was first married, whenever I laughed, my husband interpreted my laughter as ridicule. He still has a hard time understanding why I laugh, but he's gotten used to it. And when he's uncertain, he asks me to interpret.

John S. Savage suggests that we can use a perception check to be sure that we understand the feelings behind the words (*Listening and Caring Skills in Ministry: A Guide for Pastors, Counselors, and Small Group Leaders;* Abingdon Press, 1996). We begin with a tentative statement so that we don't imply that we know definitely what the person means. Then we add the feeling we think is being expressed and the reason for the feeling. For example, we might say to a kindergarten child, "I got the feeling that you were angry (or unhappy or upset) when I didn't ask you to help serve the juice. Is that right?"

When we recognize the feelings of the speaker, we are expressing our concern and interest in that person. According to Savage, when communication is flowing freely between all group members, we are more likely to achieve emotional health. By creating a safe place to articulate feelings without hurting others, we are building a strong, trusting Christian community.

## IN TOUCH THROUGH MENTORING

When teachers and group leaders are paying attention to their group members, understanding the way they express themselves, and listening for the important issues in their lives, they become partners with God in creating an environment in which people can grow and learn. In an atmosphere of trust, acceptance, and caring, teachers serve as spiritual friends to those with whom they teach and learn.

Spiritual friendship is a gift from God, binding people together. When we attend to the joys and concerns of others, we begin to see how God is present and active in their lives. We help them recognize God's gracious presence and discover ways to respond. As we interact with one another over time, we come to understand the gifts and graces each brings to our common life. We become one in the Spirit of Christ.

This oneness should not be confused with sameness. Spiritual friendship creates space for questions. Mentors (spiritual friends) ask questions as they help group members reflect on their experience in light of Scripture and the Christian tradition. Mentors also feel comfortable with questions and doubts. They welcome experimentation and testing of new ideas, concepts, and practices.

As teachers listen to group members, they begin to understand their deepest yearnings. They help in articulating individuals' visions for their lives. They help in discerning the meaning of life as part of the body of Christ.

In community we form our identity as beloved children of God. Our spiritual friends mirror that image for us and help us to see ourselves in that image. Mentors recognize our potential and inherent worth. They invite us to explore our potential and live out of our sense of worth.

Long-term relationships with people of influence, integrity, and compassion help us continue to grow into the image of Christ. These relationships, then, take the shape of a journey. Our classes and small groups cease to be settings for an institutional agenda. They become arenas for God's activity. Spiritual friends are our companions along the way.

Mentors in the faith become representatives of God's grace for others. Through their attitudes, actions, values, and beliefs, spiritual friends offer an incarnational experience of the faith. They model for us what it is like to be Christian community. They help open our eyes, ears, and heart to God. They help us recognize the truth of Bonhoeffer's statement: "We belong to one another only through and in Jesus Christ" (Life Together, by Dietrich Bonhoeffer; © 1954 HarperCollins Publishers, Inc.; page 21).

# GUIDE FOR GROUP USE

1. Read aloud the quote from Dietrich Bonhoeffer on page 55. Talk about what you think Bonhoeffer meant when he said that we belong to one another.

2. Invite a certified leader to administer the Myers-Briggs Type Indicator® to your education or nurture ministry team and/or in your adult Sunday school classes and small groups. Ask the leader to interpret the results for your teachers. Discuss ways to incorporate what they learn into their classes and small groups.

3. In your education or nurture ministry team, identify a group of people to interview in the coming months. Prepare for the interviews by practicing with one another the perception checks and paraphrasing. You might want to create an interview form with the questions you will ask and space for recording responses.

4. With your teachers and small-group leaders, think about the people who have served as spiritual friends for you and for them. Ask them to divide into groups of two or three for discussion. After everyone has had a chance to talk, ask participants to reflect on the stories they told. Make a list of the characteristics of a spiritual friend. Discuss how you, as teachers and leaders, can serve as spiritual friends in your congregation.

# chapter 4

# Keeping in Touch With Your Experience

*Do not be conformed to this world, but be transformed by the renewing of your minds, so that you may discern what is the will of God—what is good and acceptable and perfect.*

*Romans 12:2*

In Chapter 1 we considered Loren Mead's description of the shifts within the culture and the church's relationship to the culture. We noted that we continue to experience the collapse of the Christendom Era in which Christianity was firmly established as the reigning expression of faith. We continue to experience the decline of the Christian faith's authority in influencing societal norms and agendas. We live in an increasingly secular society. Diversity and pluralism, including religious pluralism, are here to stay.

We must continually remind ourselves that we can no longer assume that every person in the church has a basic understanding of the Christian faith. Members and critics of The United Methodist Church frequently complain that they don't think the denomination stands for anything. This lament indicates a lack of knowledge about the Wesleyan and Evangelical United Brethren traditions from which we come (for example, our particular understanding of prevenient, justifying, and sanctifying grace and Wesley's concept of holiness).

In a post-Christendom, postmodern culture, it is essential for us to address the issues of Christian identity. Who are we as one faith community among many? What is distinctively Christian about our practices? How do we live out our identity in today's world? (In other words, what is our mission?)

Our response to these questions involves several factors. First, the context in which we live is one of the major factors in determining our response. Throughout the ages each generation, each nation, and each culture have brought their life experiences to the reading of the Scripture and the practice of their faith. We do the same today. We do not read the Bible, make decisions about how we live our faith, or worship in a vacuum. Who we are, where and how we live, and how we are treated by others all affect our understanding of the faith, our relationship with God, and our concept of ourselves.

Second, we must also pay attention to our benchmarks of authority. How do we make decisions about identity and mission? Which experiences or teachings hold the most value and credibility for us? When our experience and teaching contradict each other, how will we determine which is most authoritative?

Third, since Christian discipleship is fundamentally about the way in which we live out our faith in the world, we must also attend to the connections between our beliefs and our practice. The Christian faith blends our being (identity) and our doing (mission). The changes at every level of our society call us to reexamine how we integrate what we believe with how we live.

As we attempt to balance our context with the ongoing Christian tradition, determine what is authoritative, and discover appropriate ways to serve as Christ's disciples in the world, we must use all the resources at our disposal to begin answering these questions of identity and mission. Chapters 2 and 3 explored some of the resources we have as teachers—spiritual disciplines and tools for listening to and understanding people in our small groups. In this chapter we will turn to another resource needed for teaching and learning today: theological reflection.

In much of Protestant Christianity, theology has been the domain of professional scholars and pastors. Over the centuries, theology has become the study of religion (for us, the study of Christianity), rather than a discipline that takes seriously the connections between our faith and the world's deepest needs. Thus many of us ordinary churchgoers, living in "the real world," have found little time or inclination to expend any energy in theological reflection.

This is not necessarily surprising. During the Christendom Era, people in the church took for granted the church's power. For hundreds of years the church's position in society was stable and constant. Therefore, church members recognized little need for critical self-reflection. They perceived little or no value in communication with the world. The church could make pronouncements, as well as legislate morals and ethics.

Today the church's position in society has changed. We experience radical change in every facet of our lives. We live in a time of instability and, some would say, chaos. I hope by now that you are convinced that we are living in a time that calls for radical change in how we have been "doing church." We cannot afford to continue with business as usual.

It is time for the laity to reclaim their role as theologians. Teachers, small-group leaders, and pastors must lead this effort in order for our congregations to be equipped to engage with any integrity the world in which we live.

Theological reflection, simply put, is Christian thinking. Congregational leaders who take seriously their role as theologians will create an environment where thinking about faith is nurtured and encouraged. If our congregations are going to be places of spiritual maturity, we need teachers who are spiritually mature. We need teachers who think. Now, of course we know that all Christians think, so we can say that all of us are already theologians. What we must do is to develop a self-awareness that helps us articulate what it is we think.

Each of us holds a core set of values and beliefs. These values and beliefs shape the way we view the world and the way we interact with the world. The world and how we interact with the world shape these values and beliefs. Much of the time our actions are congruent with our values and beliefs. However, if you're like me, every once in a while you are surprised by something you have said or done. It seems to go against the grain of your stated system of beliefs and values. When that happens, you may discover what you *really* believe.

## UNDERSTANDING OUR CONTEXT

The context for our theological reflection is the world in which we live. This context includes the issues, questions, fears, and priorities of our culture. Our context is both particular and global.

As teachers, we may begin with our family, our congregation, our town, or our state. Our context also includes our nation and our world. Our context encompasses our socioeconomic status, gender, racial/ethnic background, and political persuasion.

I assume that virtually everyone who reads this book is North American. We bring to the faith our experience (our context) of living in a highly technological society that values individualism, materialism, consumerism, and competition. Many of us are descendants of early immigrants who envisioned America as a land of never-ending opportunity. We have inherited a dream of inevitable progress and success that is well deserved. And we have enshrined that dream as a goal worthy of achieving by everyone—not only here in the United States but also in all the world!

Current reality in United States society challenges those dreams and assumptions. For the first time in the history of the dominant culture in the United States, children do not necessarily expect to do as well or better financially than their parents. In this century, events such as the Holocaust have caused us to question our assumptions about the nature of humanity and the inevitability of progress. The time-honored keys to success in our culture—a good education, good job, happy marriage and family—are not necessarily available to everyone. Even when they are attained, they no longer guarantee success.

This reality, incomplete as it may be and inapplicable to some as it may be, is our context, our story. It is as our story intersects with the biblical story that we discover God's active presence in the world and in our lives. Because we believe in a God who acts in and through the world, we must participate in the world. Christianity is not a spectator sport. Our faith offers us hope in the face of pain and confusion. Our faith gives us a particular viewpoint with which to evaluate the world and its values.

Our faith does not call us to remove ourselves from the world. Rather, we are called to participate in an ongoing dialogue with the world. This dialogue includes what the world has to say to us as Christians and what we as the Christian church have to say to the world. While the world cannot set the agenda for the church, the church can receive needed feedback and input from the world.

The biblical record of God's creative activity begins with the words: "In the beginning when God created the heavens and the earth" (Genesis 1:1). John's gospel reminds us: "For God so loved the world that he gave his only Son, so that everyone who believes in him may not perish but may have eternal life" (John 3:16). At the close of the biblical record, we read:

> Then I saw a new heaven and a new earth; for the first heaven and the first earth had passed away, and the sea was no more. And I saw the holy city, the new Jerusalem, coming down out of heaven from God, prepared as a bride adorned for her husband. And I heard a loud voice from the throne saying, "See, the home of God is among mortals. He will dwell with them; they will be his peoples, and God himself will be with them."
>
> (Revelation 21:1-3)

As they say in ecclesiastic circles, that'll preach! Do you hear the great love God has for us and for our world? Do you hear God's call to share in that love? Our faith, the Christian faith, is love in action. It is engagement in the world in the name of Christ, the One who gave himself in order that all might have life. This is our Christian vocation.

By now you might be thinking, *All right all ready! I should reflect theologically on my context. So how do I go about it?* Douglas John Hall, author of *Thinking the Faith: Christian Theology in a North American Context* (Fortress Press, 1991), suggests four questions to get us started:

1. Who are the victims of our society?
2. How do the most reflective members of our society perceive our context?
3. What do we discover by comparing our society's values and goals with the values and goals identified by our authoritative sources?
4. Within the community of faith, how does our dialogue critique our culture?

Each of these questions calls us to self-awareness and truthfulness. If you are like me, the inequities and injustices that exist—not only in the world at large but also in our communities and families—can overwhelm you. Hall identifies at least three possible responses. We may feel hopeless, which leads to despair. We may refuse to acknowledge the evidence of pain and suffering around us, which leads to self-deception. Or we may be realistic without becoming immobilized.

Theological reflection is ultimately a matter of spiritual discernment. Through prayerful study of the Scriptures and our tradition, we find the courage to address the issues facing us each day. We are able to witness to the ultimate triumph of God's grace and purpose for the world. Without diminishing the seriousness of the challenges before us, we seek the Spirit's guidance in speaking a word of life to a hurting and needy world.

## RECOGNIZING AUTHORITY

Our theological task is not only to reflect on our context but also to articulate our beliefs and discover the roots of these beliefs. Many of our beliefs spring from a variety of sources. These sources may include our parents, teachers, pastors or other church leaders, psychology and the other social sciences, plus many more. Not all the sources for our beliefs are Christian in origin. We may find occasionally that the beliefs we hold in the secret recesses of our hearts are actually contradicted by the Christian faith.

As Christians, we want to demonstrate integrity in our beliefs and actions. None of us wants to live by the motto "Do as I say, not as I do." It is therefore necessary for us to test our beliefs and our actions for consistency and faithfulness to the gospel.

John Wesley believed that we should judge our beliefs in light of Scripture, tradition, experience, and reason. These four norms, as well as other sources, help us identify what is authoritative for us. Let's consider how we, as teachers, can engage these four norms in our theological reflection.

## Scripture

The revelation of God found in the Bible is the primary story for us as Christian teachers. As we read and study Scripture, we encounter the Word of God. As Christians, we believe that we have access to the presence of God through the Old and New Testaments. As we deepen our knowledge of the Scripture, its stories impact our understanding of God, the world, and ourselves.

In 1968 The Methodist Church and The Evangelical United Brethren Church united to form The United Methodist Church. The foundational documents of both former denominations affirm that the Bible contains all that is "necessary to salvation." That affirmation attributes to Scripture primary authority for our faith and practice. (See *The Book of Discipline of The United Methodist Church*, 1996, for the complete text of the Articles of Religion of The Methodist Church and the Confession of Faith of The Evangelical United Brethren Church.)

Within the Scriptures we discover the fundamental message of the Christian faith: God was in Christ reconciling the world to God's self. Through Christ we are forgiven and are made whole. In Christ we are called to be agents of reconciliation in the world. This is the good news that inspires us, guides us, and captures our imagination.

The biblical witness provides us with a vision of life within the Christian community. We also envision what it means to be Christ's disciples in the world. Theological reflection encourages an ongoing

dialogue with this witness. As we reflect on the Scriptures, we interpret their meaning for our lives today. We are challenged to discover
ways to live that are faithful to that meaning.

The Bible provides a lens through which we can judge our experience. This is not an exercise in finding isolated verses to justify our
actions or beliefs to ourselves. We must be well versed in the Scriptures, so that we know the overarching themes that represent how God
has been known and understood. We must be aware of the whole picture of God's relationship with human beings. We test our assumptions
about God against the biblical images of God. That means that we must
study the whole Bible, not just our favorite parts. Otherwise, there is
danger of limited vision, misconceptions, and self-deceit.

Teachers must practice this kind of serious biblical study if they
hope to encourage their group members to do so. As we study the
Scripture and read the Bible devotionally, we open ourselves to an
encounter with the living God. This encounter transforms us, sustains us, and prepares us for engagement with the world.

Our personal experience of God's grace creates within us the
passion for communicating the gospel to others. We know that our
witness alone cannot guarantee a similar experience for our group
members. However, our witness certainly will have more power
than it would without enthusiasm or conviction. Those of us who
teach must create learning environments that encourage in-depth
study of the Bible and critical reflection on its meaning for our
practice of Christian discipleship.

## Tradition

We have a rich heritage as Christians. As we read in Hebrews
12:1: "We are surrounded by so great a cloud of witnesses." Even if
we are unaware of the most famous Christian writers, thinkers, and
practitioners from the past, we have been shaped by their thoughts,
their patterns of worship, and their interpretations of the faith. We
did not create the gospel; it is a gift from God, passed down from
those who have come before us.

Christian tradition may be described as the reservoir of the church's teaching about God and God's activity in Jesus Christ. Tradition includes, but is not limited to, the Scriptures. It also includes our hymns, creeds, symbols, rituals, and faith language.

There is much that we, as United Methodists, hold in common with other Christian denominations. With our sisters and brothers in Christ, we believe in the following:

- the Trinity (Creator, Redeemer, and Sustainer)
- the gift of salvation through Jesus Christ
- justification by grace through faith
- the authority of Scripture
- the reign of God, present and future

United Methodists also hold some distinct doctrines, including:

- prevenient, justifying, and sanctifying grace
- the balance of faith and works (works of piety and works of mercy)

Christian tradition is vitally connected to Christian identity. When we choose to identify ourselves with the Christian community, we choose to participate in an ongoing, particular way of living and being in the world that has roots in the past and a vision for the future. Until recently it was not unusual to consider *American* and *Christian* to be synonyms. Therefore, many Americans who identify themselves as Christian do so without having made any conscious choice to follow the example of Christ. While Christianity has definitely influenced American culture, we know that being an American does not automatically make one a Christian. As teachers and theologians, we must attempt to sort out which parts of our tradition are distinctively Christian tradition and which are cultural tradition.

I am not suggesting that tradition should be confused with rigid adherence to irrelevant rules and practices. Tradition is not worship of the past; that would be idolatry. Nor should the authority of tradition be translated to mean "We've always done it that way and we always will." In fact, Wesley used tradition as a way to critique the practices of the church of his day, rather than as a way to maintain the status quo.

For purposes of theological reflection, we use tradition in dialogue with Scripture, reason, and our experience to discern the call of God and determine appropriate responses to that call. Tradition is one of the reminders that we are in community with other Christians as we seek to be obedient and faithful to God's leading. It is authoritative because it continues to speak to contemporary society in meaningful ways.

Let me tell a personal story. For nine years my husband served in the United States Navy. We lived in Japan for three of those years. While we were there, I was active in the chapel services on base. While they were "generic" Protestant services, they were not much different from the United Methodist worship services to which I was accustomed. I learned a few new hymns and recited some new prayers. But for the most part, I was unaware of any drastic changes in my worship experience.

After we returned to the United States, I began working in a United Methodist congregation again. On the first Sunday that I participated in the Lord's Supper, I was totally unprepared for the power of the experience. I heard for the first time in three years the words that had been spoken to me again and again since early childhood: "On the same night that Jesus was betrayed, he took bread, gave thanks, broke the bread, and gave it to his disciples, saying, 'Take, eat; this is my body which is given for you.'"

The tears began to pour down my face. To tell the truth, I still cry whenever I tell that story. Suddenly, I knew without a doubt that I was home. Not just in a familiar place. Not just back in the "good ol' US of A." I had returned to my spiritual roots, and I knew I was home.

That is what tradition can do for us. It creates home—a place where we are known and loved, a place where we are invited to community. Tradition can be a doorway to the holy. When it is, it lends authenticity to our experience and offers us guidance for reflecting on that experience.

## Experience

In some ways, we have already discussed experience in the above conversation related to context. Our experience emerges from our context and shapes how we view the world and how we choose to interact with others.

From a Wesleyan perspective, experience specifically refers to religious experience, particularly our experience of new birth in Christ. Robin Maas asks whether it is possible for the Christian church to identify a common or core religious experience (By What Authority: A Conversation on Teaching Among United Methodists; edited by Elizabeth Box Price and Charles R. Foster; Abingdon Press, 1991). She then hypothesizes that it is possible. Using the church's historical teaching, based in Scripture, she identifies that core experience as a direct encounter with the risen Christ, which calls us to self-surrender and forms the basis for faithful discipleship.

This core experience "confirms" the teachings of Scripture and Christian tradition about how God has been and is now active in the lives of human beings. Wesley certainly believed that Christians must not merely adhere to a stated set of beliefs about God. He knew that it is experience that brings to life and embodies what we say we believe and what we teach in worship and through Christian education.

A case in point: Several summers ago my son Jeremy attended a week of church camp. He came home singing all the songs he had learned during the week. Many of the songs were related to the Holy Spirit, and, apparently, the camp counselors had talked with the campers about the Holy Spirit. Jeremy obviously enjoyed the lively rhythm of the songs, and he had appreciated the way in which the counselors related to the campers.

However, as he continued to talk about his week, he suddenly stopped. He looked at me and asked, "Have you ever felt the Holy Spirit?" When I answered affirmatively, he simply said, "Tell me about it." Jeremy blessed me with the opportunity to connect what I had been taught and what I had experienced. His invitation gave me the chance to share with him the reality of the presence of God in my life.

Our experience of the risen Christ unites us with all those who confess Jesus as Lord. This unity as the body of Christ is celebrated and sealed in baptism. As our faith journey unfolds, we attempt to

align all of our personal experiences with the transforming experience of God's grace, ever present and available to us. Maas reminds
us that the goal of the Christian life is more than receiving forgiveness and more than living a good life. It is, according to Wesley,
holiness of heart and life.

At this point I would like to point out the possible dichotomy
that exists within our congregations regarding religious experience.
I remind you of the diversity of spiritual types described in Chapter 3.
People who access knowledge about God through their feelings are
quite comfortable with considering religious experience as authoritative in our theological reflection. They may be critical of or
sympathetic to those who exhibit no evidence of such personal
experience.

Those of us who tend to "know" God through our thinking may
be distrustful of that which cannot be readily explained with logical
thought processes. For us, religious experience may smack of feel-
good, warm and fuzzy (emphasis on the fuzzy) theology.

Not surprisingly, this dichotomy is false. Religious experience
includes both thinking and feeling, doing and being. The validity of
religious experience is based on how that experience moves us
toward authenticity and integrity as faithful Christians.

## Reason

Reason brings to theological reflection a disciplined inquiry in
order that we might love God with all our minds. The community of
faith engages in thoughtful reflection in order to discern what is
idolatrous and what is faithful.

In today's world, we often equate reason with rational thought
and logic. John B. Cobb, Jr., author of Becoming a Thinking Christian
(Abingdon Press, 1993), disagrees with this assumption. He asserts
that reason is more about depth of understanding, clarity of thought,
and comprehensiveness in scope. Cobb's statement supports Wesley's
understanding of the role and function of reason.

John Wesley, who lived during the Age of Enlightenment, frequently
appealed to reason as a norm for Christian faith and practice. However,

he was aware that it did not function in the same capacity as Scripture, tradition, and experience. He considered reason to be a tool for our use in understanding and interpreting the Bible, Christian tradition, and our experience.

In his sermon "The Case of Reason Impartially Considered," Wesley suggested that reason consists of three components. The first is "simple apprehension." On this level, reason takes note of information or data. The second function is "judgment." When we use reason in this way, we process new information, comparing it with what we already know. We begin to categorize the new information according to previous information. Wesley described the third component of reason as "discourse." At this stage, we not only sort and categorize new information but also evaluate the relationship between the old and new data. We synthesize new ideas with old data. We are capable of identifying problems and developing strategies to address the problems. New learning begins to emerge.

For the purposes of this chapter, I suggest that it is this third component of reason that most directly relates to theological reflection. As we study the Bible, reflect on our experiences and the experiences of others in today's world, and engage in dialogue with Christian tradition, we use our reason to identify and test Christian values and practices appropriate for today. With our minds we consider new possibilities for living as Christians in today's world.

When we are tempted to avoid difficult issues, particularly those with the ability to divide us and hurt us, our reason helps us "stay at the table," working to examine the issues, explore possible courses of action, and wrestle with the questions. Reason evokes our creativity and imagination as we reflect on our present reality and dream about our future possibilities.

## MAKING THE CONNECTIONS

Christian discipleship is participation in God's continuing activity in the world. Why am I mentioning *activity* in a chapter on theological reflection? If theological reflection does not have an impact on our actions, then it is simply "a noisy gong or a clanging cymbal" (1 Corinthians 13:1).

As we reflect on Scripture and tradition (do theological reflection), we enhance our ability to view our world through the lens of faith. As we strengthen our ability to analyze the problems facing us today, we grow in our awareness of the need for change. As we increase our ability to perceive the presence and activity of God in the world around us and in our lives, we discover new ways to participate in ministry. As we worship and learn together, we build shared meaning and find affirmation and support for our common life and mission.

Earlier in this chapter, I said that theological reflection is ultimately a matter of spiritual discernment. When we, as teachers, engage in theological reflection, we are seeking to discover how God is active in the world and in our lives. We discern the ways in which God is calling us to be in ministry in our family, congregation, and community.

As we join with others in our community of faith, we discover meaning in the present and hope for the future. As teacher-theologians, we stand with the prophets of old to proclaim:

> O LORD, you are my God;
> I will exalt you, I will praise your name;
> for you have done wonderful things…
> For you have been a refuge to the poor,
>    a refuge to the needy in their distress,
>    a shelter from the rainstorm
>       and a shade from the heat.
>                                        (Isaiah 25:1, 4)

As we connect our thoughts with our actions, we perceive the relationship between our theological reflection and accountability for our Christian discipleship.

# GUIDE FOR GROUP USE

1.  How do you understand yourself as a theologian? What sources inform and shape your theological reflection?

2.  With your education or nurture ministry team or with a group of teachers, make a list of issues facing your congregation and community. Explore biblical passages and church traditions that can help you develop a strategy for interpreting and responding to the issues (for example, prayers or statements from *The Book of Discipline of The United Methodist Church, 1996*).

3.  Sponsor a series of small-group sessions on the authority of Scripture, tradition, experience, and reason. Pay particular attention to helping participants recognize how they use (or might begin to use) each of these norms in their Christian faith and practice. (Resist using these sessions as an attempt to indoctrinate group members with your particular perspective on authority.)

4.  Study Charles R. Foster's book *Educating Congregations: The Future of Christian Education* (Abingdon Press, 1994) to identify and implement strategies for educational ministries that build shared meaning and nurture hope within your small groups and congregation.

5.  Select a book about spiritual disciplines from the bibliography, on page 109. As you study the book with a small group of teachers, ministry team members, or in an existing adult class, discuss the relationship between spiritual disciplines and theological reflection.

# chapter 5

# KEEPING IN TOUCH WITH THE WORLD

*You are the light of the world. A city built on a hill cannot be hid. No one after lighting a lamp puts it under the bushel basket, but on the lampstand, and it gives light to all in the house. In the same way, let your light shine before others, so that they may see your good works and give glory to your Father in heaven.*

*Matthew 5:14-16*

Jesus calls us to be the "light of the world." What an awesome responsibility. As partners with God, we work toward the transformation of our world into what God intends the world to be. That is our Christian vocation.

We might verbalize this call as participation in the mission and ministry of the church. That sounds somewhat more manageable. Yet, however we word it, there is no escaping the fact that as Christians, we have a responsibility to live out our faith in the world. Our identity is fundamentally linked with our mission.

We have already discussed in the first chapter the mission of the church. To briefly restate it here: The mission of the church is to share the gospel of Jesus Christ with whomever we come in contact. The particular ways in which we participate in this mission will vary from congregation to congregation and from person to person.

Obviously, one of the ways we participate as small-group leaders or teachers is through teaching and leading. However, that should not be our only avenue of service. Our leadership in small groups helps to equip members of the community of faith to live as Christian disciples. In addition to service within the congregation, we must also seek ways to serve the needs of the larger community.

In this chapter we will explore the issue of accountability for our Christian discipleship. For some of us, the word *accountability* conjures up all sorts of negative images. We really don't want other people to tell us what to do. As we shall see, accountability from a Christian perspective is more closely related to an internally focused spiritual life than it is to an externally imposed authority.

The issue of Christian accountability has been widely discussed (even debated) since biblical times. At the heart of the issue is the relationship between grace and responsibility.

Many of the theological debates regarding this issue have revolved around the following:

- the basis of salvation
- the question of free will
- the purpose of good works
- the nature of God's grace

Perhaps it is a good idea to begin by acknowledging that one of the basic assumptions of the Christian faith is that human sin separates us from God and from one another. Therefore, we need to be reconciled with God and with one another. This cannot be accomplished through our own efforts. We believe that through Christ we are forgiven of sin. In Christ our relationships with God and one another are restored. John Wesley and others described this as justification.

The issues highlighted above all deal with how we "obtain" salvation. Wesley, as has already been stated, was clear that we are justified by faith alone. There are no doctrines to which we must agree in order to be in a saving relationship with God. There is no standard of behavior to which we must adhere in order to be in a relationship with God. Because God has created us and loves us, God graciously offers us the opportunity to be in relationship with him (Ephesians 2:8-9).

If justification resulted from something we are able to do, then, according to Wesley (and to Paul, Jesus, and the prophets before him), we would be operating under a system of legalism. We would still be subject to the law, as understood by the Jewish religious leaders of Jesus' day. We could not be assured of God's pardon and acceptance, because we could never be sure that we had done enough of the "right" things.

If, however, justification is solely a gift of God's grace, then we can indeed trust in God's forgiveness and love. All God requires of us in order to be saved is to accept God's gift. This response is an act of our human will. As United Methodists, we believe that God has given us freedom to accept or reject God's offer of relationship. If we have free will, then we must assume responsibility for our response.

Human responsibility might be described as the flip side of God's grace. This is a significant corrective for those of us who might mis-understand God's justifying grace. We might be tempted to ask: If we are not saved by any efforts of our own, does that mean we can do whatever we please? Are there any limits to human freedom? If God forgives us because of God's graciousness, are we at liberty to com-mit sin, assuming that we will be forgiven?

The apostle Paul and Wesley both echo a resounding "No!" Paul writes to the church at Rome:

> What then are we to say? Should we continue in sin in order that grace may abound? By no means! How can we who died to sin go on living in it? Do you not know that all of us who have been baptized into Christ Jesus were baptized into his death? There-fore we have been buried with him by baptism into death, so that, just as Christ was raised from the dead by the glory of the Father, so we too might walk in newness of life.
>
> (Romans 6:1-4)

As forgiven and reconciled people, we are called to have the mind of Christ, which compels us to be servants to others (Philippians 2:4-8). Following Christ leads to concrete actions. We will participate in good works—feeding the hungry, tending the sick and poor, and welcoming the stranger and the outcast.

Our service, our good works, are a response to God's grace, not the impetus for receiving God's grace. They are the "fruits" of our faith. Good works, which follow justification, are acts of obedience, rather than of obligation. Our deeds are born out of gratitude, rather than out of fear. They are marks of Christian discipline and maturity.

Wesley linked good works to God's sanctifying grace, to what he called "going on to perfection." Good works are an outward sign of our inward "holiness of heart." They are a natural consequence of being in relationship with God. Just as God's justifying grace brought us into relationship with God through Christ, God's sanctifying grace creates in us the will for faithful obedience through the power of the Holy Spirit.

It can be easy to get bogged down in what sounds like church jargon when we talk about things such as justification and sanctification. The important point here is the practicality of Wesley's theology. He believed that God calls us into relationship with him and empowers us to live faithfully within that relationship. That relationship takes practical, specific shape through our actions, as well as through our beliefs.

Wesley often used the image of a house to help his parishioners understand God's grace. He likened God's prevenient grace, which is at work in us even before we are aware of it, to the porch of a house. He described God's justifying grace as entering the house through the front door. It is God's sanctifying grace that helps us make the house our home, the place where we belong and where we live. Any of us who have moved to a new house know that it takes a while for us to feel at home. This ongoing process of making our spiritual "home" with God is the work of God's sanctifying grace.

## ACCOUNTABILITY AND CHRISTIAN FORMATION

As Christians, we should be seeking to deepen our relationship with God. We should be exploring how we might better serve humanity and protect the natural world. We might describe this accountability as focus and as discipline.

## Maintaining Our Focus

I participate in a weekly study and prayer group at work. Last fall we read and discussed the Gospel of Matthew. One of the week's assigned readings covered the ninth chapter. Over the course of the past several months, I have continued to turn to that chapter as an example of how focused on doing the will of God Jesus was.

Here is a brief rundown of the incidents in this chapter:

- Jesus healed a paralyzed man, who was brought to him by the man's friends.
- Jesus called Matthew, the tax collector, to follow him.
- Jesus ate dinner with "many tax collectors and sinners."
- Jesus raised a synagogue leader's daughter from the dead.
- Jesus (while on his way to see the religious leader's daughter) healed a woman who was suffering from twelve years of hemorrhaging.
- Jesus restored sight to two blind men.
- Jesus cast out a demon.
- Jesus taught in the synagogues, "proclaiming the good news of the kingdom."
- Jesus cured "every disease and every sickness."

Observing these deeds of Jesus, the Pharisees and other religious folks continually challenged him. They accused him of blasphemy (for daring to forgive the paralyzed man's sins) and of breaking the law (for eating with people who were "unclean"). They criticized him for not fasting like the other good religious folks did.

Jesus was one busy guy! I was exhausted just reading the chapter! But more importantly, I began to catch a glimpse of Jesus' steadfast commitment to obeying God. To his critics he responded: "Those who are well have no need of a physician, but those who are sick. Go and learn what this means, 'I desire mercy, not sacrifice'" (Matthew 9:12-13). To those who called upon his mercy, he offered compassion, "because they were harassed and helpless, like sheep without a shepherd" (Matthew 9:36).

Mercy, compassion, healing, forgiveness—these were the daily gifts of Jesus to those he met. And he never let his critics steer him off his chosen course. After his baptism, he had spent forty days in the wilderness clarifying God's will for his life. (See Luke 4:1-13 for one account of Jesus' wilderness experience.) Once he began his public ministry, Jesus did not waver from what he believed God intended him to do.

John Wesley was also a man of focus. In fact, as I'm sure you know, the name Methodist was a derogatory term used by Wesley's acquaintances who considered his methodical use of spiritual disciplines to be extreme.

As the Methodist movement grew, Wesley developed the General Rules to guide those who were also seeking to stay focused in the exercise of their discipleship. According to these rules, members of the Methodist societies were to

- do no harm (which included avoiding evil);
- do all the good possible to do (which included physical, as well as spiritual, assistance);
- attend all the "ordinances of God" (understood to be the means of grace described in Chapter 2).

David Lowes Watson, through his work with Covenant Discipleship groups and Class Leaders, has provided us with a contemporary understanding of this kind of focus (Forming Christian Disciples: The Role of Covenant Discipleship and Class Leaders in the Congregation; Discipleship Resources, 1995). Watson identifies individual and corporate dimensions of loving God and loving neighbor, which build on Wesley's understanding of "works of piety" and "works of mercy."

The individual dimension of "works of piety" includes "acts of devotion" (prayer, Bible study, fasting). The corporate dimension includes "acts of worship" (participation in the ministry of word and sacrament). The individual dimension of "works of mercy" includes "acts of compassion" (response to human need around the world). As the body of Christ, we carry out "acts of justice" (working to change the systems, policies, and structures that maintain inequities and injustice between people). The figure below provides a graphic illustration of this concept.

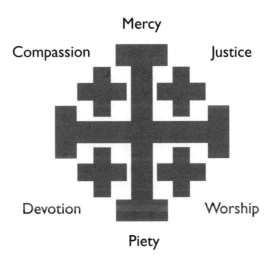

As teachers, we need to maintain a focus on our discipleship. We should develop and implement a plan for spiritual growth (personal prayer and Bible study) and participate in congregational worship. In this way we express our love for God and continue to grow in our ability to discern God's presence and guidance.

We should also seek opportunities to love our neighbors as ourselves by expressing compassion and working for justice (Mark 12:31). These opportunities may be as formal as regularly visiting the residents of a nursing home, helping build a house through Habitat for Humanity, or sponsoring a letter-writing campaign to advocate healthcare reform. We should also be attentive to the informal opportunities we have to show kindness to the people we encounter each day. We can demonstrate patience, rather than irritation, when we're waiting in traffic or standing in line at the bank. We can take the time to listen to a teenager from down the street. We can shop for a friend when we learn he or she is ill.

Since the needs of the world are so numerous, we have plenty of opportunities to practice our discipleship. As we stay focused on God's call to servanthood, we will discover the gifts we have received from God for service. As we continue to practice the spiritual disciplines, we will discover anew the reality of God's grace in our lives and in the world around us. In both our practice and in our reflection, we will continue the dance of grace and responsibility.

## Leading a Disciplined Life

One of the keys to the success of the early Methodist movement was the way in which Wesley organized people into small groups for support in their Christian journey. He understood that people needed encouragement, fellowship, and assistance as they sought to be faithful disciples. Wesley was convinced that Christian discipleship could best be nurtured through an accountable fellowship.

There were several kinds of groups that one could join. The first was one of the Methodist societies. A society might be a fairly large group. Membership was open to anyone who sought to live a holy life through obedience to Christ and was willing to abide by the rules of the society. The societies met once a week for prayer, confession, preaching, and mutual support.

Societies were divided into classes, which also met on a weekly basis. These smaller groups tended to include people living within the same neighborhood. Members met with a class leader for spiritual discernment and for sharing the joys and struggles of their spiritual lives. The class leader, whom Wesley appointed, was responsible for knowing well the members of the class. He or she asked each class member questions based on the General Rules. The class member would respond to the questions as a way of reporting on the state of his or her spiritual life. The class leader would then give advice based on what he or she heard.

Those Christians demonstrating a certain level of maturity also might participate in a "band." While membership in a class was mandatory for all society members, membership in a band was optional. These were single-sex small groups of from five to ten women or men who met for fellowship and support. Each band chose its own leader from among its members. The structure of the bands was less formal than that of the class meetings. However, the nature of the conversation was generally more personal and intensive. They focused on advanced spiritual growth.

Sometimes individual members of a class or band would write a personal covenant as a statement of their intent to live in faithful response to God's grace. The covenant would cover aspects of their spiritual life in which they knew they particularly needed to grow. According to David Lowes Watson, these "covenants were a mark of maturity, an expression on the part of seasoned disciples that something was needed to sustain them in their journey" (*The Early Methodist Class Meeting: Its Origins and Significance;* © 1985 Discipleship Resources, Nashville, Tennessee; page 38). While the classes became the basic unit of the Methodist movement, each of these group settings shared several common characteristics:

- sharing of religious experience through testimonies
- quest for personal holiness and growth in grace
- self-examination
- commitment to freedom of opinion
- "watching over one another in love"

## ACCOUNTABILITY IN TODAY'S WORLD

It is no less difficult to live as Christian disciples today than it was in Wesley's day. Teachers, pastors, and other congregational leaders must find support and encouragement in order to serve as the spiritual leaders God has called them to be.

As a teacher, what kind of a support system do you have in place? Who are the spiritually mature Christians on whom you can depend and whose advice you seek? How often do you need to meet with those people in order to stay on track? What resources have you found helpful in developing your spiritual life? How are you regularly participating in service to your community?

As you consider these questions, remember that each of us is unique. Your plan for spiritual growth and accountability will not be the same as mine. My plan will not be a replica of another teacher's in my congregation.

Here are some possibilities for putting a plan in place:

- Organize a small group of teachers (or friends) to meet for prayer and Bible study. Agree to meet for several months. Then evaluate your progress and decide what next steps you need to take.

- Join a Covenant Discipleship group in your congregation. If there isn't a group available, ask your pastor about beginning one. Or find a similar group in your workplace or neighborhood. For more information about Covenant Discipleship groups, write to: Director of Accountable Discipleship, The General Board of Discipleship, P.O. Box 840, Nashville, TN 37202-0840.

- Locate a spiritual director or other mentor who will meet with you on an individual basis for discussing your spiritual growth and providing insight and direction for continued maturity.

- Participate in a DISCIPLE Bible study class in order to enhance your understanding of the Bible and the call to Christian discipleship.

- Identify your local community's version of Meals on Wheels. Volunteer to deliver meals to homebound people several times a month.

- Pray and read the Bible with your family on a daily basis. Talk about how your family can witness to your faith in your community. Support one another's desire to grow in faith.

- Lend your efforts to an after-school tutoring program for children or youth.

- Correspond with a Christian in another community. (If it's available, don't forget e-mail.) As you communicate perspectives on living as disciples, support one another with advice, prayer, and encouragement.

Whatever you decide to do, know that God will be with you. Through God's grace we live in relationship with God and one another. Through God's Spirit we continue to grow in that grace.

# GUIDE FOR GROUP USE

1. Discuss the relationship between grace and responsibility. Explore the role of good works in Christian discipleship. Be open to opinions that differ from your own. Encourage open, honest sharing.
2. Review the descriptions of the early Methodist societies, class meetings, and bands (pages 80–81). Pay particular attention to the functions of these groups. Then review the opportunities for mutual accountability offered by your congregation. Identify any gaps and develop strategies for eliminating them.
3. Read Philippians 2:1-11. Talk about what it means to have the mind of Christ. List some of the ways in which we might concretely demonstrate the mind of Christ.
4. Invite someone experienced in Covenant Discipleship groups to make a presentation to your teachers. Explore the possibility of organizing Covenant Discipleship groups in your congregation.
5. Develop a mentoring program in your congregation. Identify people who are spiritually mature and who exhibit a deep love for God and for other people. Provide them with knowledge and skills for being a "friend in faith."
6. Publicize and promote opportunities for mission and service in which teachers and small-group leaders can participate. Consider organizing a work/study trip to one of the United Methodist mission sites in this country or overseas. You might want to check the General Board of Global Ministries Internet site (http://gbgm-umc.org) and request information about their mission caravans.

# chapter 6

# KEEPING IN TOUCH WITH TEACHING

*The gifts he gave were that some would be apostles, some prophets, some evangelists, some pastors and teachers, to equip the saints for the work of ministry, for building up the body of Christ.*

*Ephesians 4:11-12*

As I begin this last chapter, I am reminded of a saying we have in my family: "I said all that to say this." In some ways the saying applies to the previous chapters of this resource. The critical processes described in Chapters 2–5 are important because they help shape us into the people God intends us to be. In the context of this book, they are also significant because of the direct impact they have on the critical process of teaching and leading a small group gathered for growth in faith and discipleship.

I regard teaching as a means of grace. I believe that as people gather in Christian community to support one another, pray together, read the Bible, connect their faith with their experience, and seek to serve God and God's people, they open themselves to the presence of the living God. Those who prepare the way for others to experience this kind of Christian community are channels of God's grace.

People join classes or small groups for a variety of reasons. Some say they want to know more about the Bible. Some express a need for Christian friendship. Some want to explore a particular topic, such as parenting or United Methodist history and doctrine. Others may be committed to addressing the issues of poverty, healthcare, or homelessness. Still others may have no well-defined reason for joining a group; they attend because they think it's expected of them.

Regardless of the stated reasons people give for participating in the small-group ministries of a congregation, I believe that their desire to be connected to God and to other human beings in meaningful ways is the root of their participation. Richard Robert Osmer suggests that teaching awakens, supports, and challenges faith (*Teaching for Faith: A Guide for Teachers of Adult Classes*; Westminster John Knox Press, 1992).

The General Board of Discipleship published a book titled *Foundations: Shaping the Ministry of Christian Education in Your Congregation* (Discipleship Resources, 1993), which guides congregations in exploring their task of making disciples through teaching and learning. It describes the process of Christian formation as one in which individuals and communities of faith are transformed by God's grace as they come to

- know and experience God through Jesus Christ;
- claim and live God's promises;
- grow and serve as Christian disciples.

This statement grounds the ministry of teaching and learning within the holy mystery of God's desire to live in relationship with us.

## A DYNAMIC PROCESS

Teaching and learning for Christian formation is a dynamic process. It is a weaving together of the strands of our lives in a way that shapes our identity, illuminates our purpose, and challenges us to be all that God has intended us to be. It builds on the past, interprets our present, and imagines the future.

### Memory and Identity

Identity refers to the characteristics of a person that remain constant over the course of time. Our identity is who we are. It is shaped by our formative experiences, particularly those within our family and other significant groups. It is expressed through our commitments of time and energy. Within the community of faith, personal identity is shaped by the Christian story and customs, as well as by one's cultural location and social realities.

One of the amazing occurrences in our world during the last decade has been the collapse of Communism and the revitalization of the Christian church in many of the former Communist countries. A friend of mine, Marilyn Beecher, spent three years in Bulgaria working with The United Methodist Church there. While she was there she was asked by the General Board of Global Ministries to write an article for one of their mission magazines about Christmas in Bulgaria. In order to meet her writing deadline, Marilyn had to interview Bulgarian Methodists during the month of July.

In her article she told of traveling to a small town several hours from Sofia to meet with a group of Bulgarian Christians. When she asked them to tell about some of the Bulgarian Christmas customs, their countenances fell. They bowed their heads and looked very sad. They told Marilyn that it had been so long since they had been allowed to celebrate Christmas that they weren't sure they could remember. Then suddenly one of the men looked up and said, "I do remember a song. Do you know this song?" And there in the middle of summer, he began to sing in Bulgarian "Silent Night, Holy Night."

Marilyn's poignant depiction of these faithful Christians illustrates the vital role that memory plays in building individual and communal identity. We are a people with good news: God has come in Jesus Christ so that we might be God's people!

Every week when we gather for worship, study, and fellowship, we rehearse through story, symbol, and ritual who we are and whose we are. Throughout the church year we hear the stories that have shaped us as Christians for two thousand years. Regularly we gather around the table to remember the One who is "the bread of life" and who calls us to extend his ministry throughout the world.

Memory grounds our present in the central events of the past that have made us who we are. Sometimes, as the church in Bulgaria illustrates, it is memory alone that gives us hope for the future.

Linda J. Vogel puts it this way:

> We cannot imagine a future without remembering our past. Our sense of identity (who and whose we are), our personal and communal stories, and all that gives life meaning are bound up in our gift of memory (*Teaching and Learning in Communities of Faith: Empowering Adults Through Religious Education*; © 1991 Jossey-Bass Publishers; page 28).

Teaching the faith involves building a storehouse of memory. Memory, in an educational context, is not static; it does not hold us in the past. Rather, it serves as a catalyst for evaluating our current reality and discerning meaning. As we learn together, we build shared meaning, claim our shared identity, and participate in our shared ministry.

## Identity and Vision

The gospel of Jesus Christ is a proclamation of the good news of the kingdom. It is a declaration of God's vision for the world. It is a vision grounded in the prophetic witness of the Hebrew Scriptures. It calls us to imagine a world where those who are hungry are fed, those who mourn are comforted, those who are sick are healed, and those who are friendless are befriended. It calls us to imagine a world where justice rolls "down like waters, and righteousness like an ever-flowing stream" (Amos 5:24).

As we encounter the creative and redemptive activity of God in the world and through our small groups, we are caught up in that vision. Effective teaching enables us to perceive new ways in which God is actively working in our world. It motivates us to envision possibilities and alternatives for the brokenness we experience around us. It challenges us to hear God's call to work with God for the fulfillment of God's vision.

Vision takes time to emerge. When we are attempting to understand, both cognitively and practically, theological concepts of justice, grace, accountability, and so forth, we can get lost in abstraction and fail to see the relevance to our daily lives. A part of the problem is the inadequacy of human language and thought to describe God.

Educator-theologians, such as Sallie McFague and Linda J. Vogel, suggest that the use of metaphors provide us with a tool for exploring God's vision for humanity and the created order. According to Vogel, metaphors "provide us with language for the journey. They introduce questions and encourage us to explore issues and ideas" (*Teaching and Learning in Communities of Faith: Empowering Adults Through Religious Education;* © 1991 Jossey-Bass Publishers; page 35). We can use metaphors to help us explain what we mean and entertain new possibilities.

As teachers, we can introduce metaphors to our group members. We can also help group members recognize the metaphors they employ to describe God's gracious activity. Some of the biblical metaphors that could help us understand God's vision include the following:

- *covenant*—God's promise to be faithful to God's Word, and our promise to serve only God;
- *the kingdom of God*—God's intended reality for the world;
- *sabbath*—calling a halt to our frenetic activity and taking the time for spiritual nourishment;
- *table*—a center of generosity, hospitality, and abundance, where everyone is welcome and no one is excluded.

Contemporary metaphors might include the following:

- *partnership*—the connection between God and humans, and human beings with one another;
- *health and wholeness*—God's desire for all people to experience abundance of life.

Whatever metaphors we choose to employ, building a common identity and shared vision is a theological and educational exercise that is rooted in God's faithfulness. We trust in God; therefore, we are people of hope.

# AN INTERACTIVE PROCESS

Teaching is a creative, interactive process that brings together a diversity of people who have disparate needs and varying beliefs. Through the grace of God, we discover unity in our diversity and learn to live as reconciled people. In order to facilitate this kind of experience, teachers must attend to a variety of factors that impact the teaching/learning setting.

## Group Members

Teachers must begin with where the people are—what they know, what they believe, what their experience has been. Group members' age, gender, personality type, and learning style will influence their expectations for and involvement in the group.

Teachers will also benefit from understanding the general age-level characteristics of the group they lead. Age-level characteristics include our mental, social, emotional, psychological, and spiritual development. Jean Piaget's research provides helpful guidelines for learning about the cognitive development of human beings. Erik Erikson's theories of psychosocial development shed light on the affective development of humans. Lawrence Kohlberg, Carol Gilligan, John Westerhoff, and James Fowler have built our knowledge of moral and faith development, particularly as it relates to decision-making, locus of authority, and breadth of perspective.

And if that's not enough to keep up with, we teachers also need to understand how people learn. This is particularly important since we tend to develop learning experiences based on our own learning style. Unless we have a group of people who are very similar to us, we will miss the mark for a lot of our group members. While curriculum resources attempt to provide a variety of learning activities that will help teachers diversify the experiences they plan, the resources will be effective only when the teacher reviews the possible activities and then selects those most appropriate for the members of her or his group.

Chapter 3 included information about personality types and spiritual types. Here we will focus on how people learn. For many years educators have known that people learn in different ways. Howard Gardner, a Harvard psychologist, believes that there has been too much importance attached to logical and verbal thinking as a measure of intelligence. This perception of intelligence has been the predominant influence over the form and content of education.

Over the past twenty years, Gardner has developed a theory he calls "multiple intelligences." In *Frames of Mind: The Theory of Multiple Intelligences* (BasicBooks, 1983), he suggests that there are at least seven ways that people process information, respond to new situations, and learn from experience. He asserts that individuals rarely use a single intelligence in isolation. Rather, they integrate a variety of the intelligences to form their own pattern of learning.

On the following page, you will find a chart that summarizes seven of the intelligences Gardner has identified. It also includes suggested implications for teaching in the church. As you read through the possible learning activities, you will see how many of the activities might relate to people with different learning preferences. For example, roleplaying may appeal to logical-mathematical intelligence because it involves problem solving. It may appeal to linguistic (verbal) intelligence since it entails speaking. It might also appeal to bodily-kinesthetic intelligence because of its use of bodily movement.

## Sacred Space

Teachers are spiritual leaders. I'm convinced of that. As we listen to God and God's people, we can discern ways to create learning environments that become sacred space. We can understand the communal nature of the Christian faith and, therefore, assume our responsibility in "building up the body of Christ" (Ephesians 4:7, 11-13). One of the ways we can do that is through committing ourselves to partnership and teamwork and encouraging shared leadership. We should foster the development of each group member's gifts and graces and lend support as he or she uses those gifts in Christ's service.

Teachers need to recognize the value of open communication, where they consistently exchange information. Since Christian

## Seven Intelligences

| Learning Preference | Description | Related Learning Activities |
|---|---|---|
| 1. Linguistic (Verbal) | Focuses on the use of language, both spoken and written | Storytelling; writing stories, prayers, or poetry; reading the Bible and church stories; class discussion and conversation; drama; praying aloud |
| 2. Spatial (Visual) | Focuses on the ability to visualize and create mental images | Drawing or painting, guided imagery, maps and graphs, looking at pictures or picture books |
| 3. Bodily-Kinesthetic | Focuses on physical movement and manipulation of objects | Dancing, sports, games, moving to music, puppets, arts and crafts |
| 4. Logical-Mathematical | Focuses on numbers, sequence, and abstract concepts and reasoning | Problem solving, learning the books of the Bible in order, puzzles, games, roleplaying |
| 5. Musical (Rhythmic) | Focuses on music, rhythms, and tones | Singing in the classroom or in a choir, listening to music, studying hymns, playing a musical instrument, writing music and/or lyrics |
| 6. Interpersonal | Focuses on collaboration and interaction between people | Cooperative learning, group projects, expressing feelings, sharing work, listening to others, expressing care |
| 7. Intrapersonal | Focuses on the inner life | Prayer, writing in a journal, silence, dealing with feelings, thinking about family issues |

formation is a lifelong process, we must develop climates that value learning from experience, as well as from study. We should seek to "capture" that learning so that learning can be shared throughout the congregation and with new members of the group.

Teachers should understand that leadership is a responsibility, not a privilege. Spiritual leadership is an offering of self for the sake of others. It is servant leadership in the name of Christ (Romans 12). While teachers have significant influence in shaping Christian community, they should be keenly aware that they, too, are shaped by their participation in group life. They should seek to be accountable to the group, just as they hold others accountable.

Teachers should invite others to discover God in the midst of everyday life. As spiritual leaders, we should be attuned to God's presence in our own lives and should be able to help others in exploring how God is at work in their lives. While we should feel comfortable in sharing our faith, we should not expect others to duplicate our faith journey.

We should seek to provide opportunities for people to seek God and to make a commitment to Christian discipleship. We can model an ongoing process of reflection that leads to continued insight and growth in faith. We should also help people identify and develop the knowledge and skills necessary for living out their commitment to God in Christ.

In *The Learning Congregation: A New Vision of Leadership* (Westminster John Knox Press, 1997), Thomas R. Hawkins explores the importance of a safe place for self-reflection. He suggests that we need space and time to contemplate our experience, relate it to prior experiences, consider possible consequences, and reflect on it in light of Scripture and through prayer in order to learn. In sacred space we are able to raise questions about the assumptions that guide our actions and test new ideas for understanding our experience and living ever more faithfully.

Teachers should create a climate of respect and honor for the diversity of God's people and should incorporate a variety of methods and tools that speak to different learning styles, temperaments, and spiritual types. They should understand the role that gender, age, and marital status play in group dynamics. They should express respect for and interest in the racial and cultural heritage of group members and should encourage group members to reflect on their heritage in dialogue with their faith.

In this climate, all people can discover their gifts and graces and can offer and receive support from other group members. They can grow in their desire to be accountable to the "body" for their discipleship. In this climate, people can safely explore who God is calling them to be and what kind of community God is calling the group to be.

Teachers should also support the health and wholeness of others in every way—physically, emotionally, mentally, psychologically, and spiritually. When we pay close attention to the health of the entire group, we are aware particularly of the impact of group life on the most vulnerable. We should understand that when a person is restored to health, that person's place in the group changes and, therefore, the group is changed. We must understand how to help a group through transition and growth. We should take seriously our role as "ambassadors for Christ" through the ministry of reconciliation (2 Corinthians 5:17-20).

In sacred space where men and women encounter the living God, discover who they are in relationship to God and one another, and find support in living their faith, they are energized and empowered for ministry. From a Wesleyan perspective, as they work out their own salvation, they find themselves traveling together on the road of sanctification, guided by their teachers.

## Content

In addition to understanding how people learn and how teachers create a learning environment that becomes sacred space for the learners, teachers are responsible for paying attention to the content of the group meetings. I am defining content to include three different dimensions: relationships, practices, and information.

Christian formation is a corporate act and responsibility by virtue of the nature of the Christian faith. We affirm that God has called us into community to be God's people. Our small groups provide opportunities for significant, deep, and challenging interaction between people that assists them in following the Great Commandment to love God and love neighbor (Mark 12:28-34).

These relationships are the heart of the teaching and learning process. Through our small groups, we should be building not only friendships but also Christian community.

The human need to be loved is powerful. Within the Christian community we have opportunities to share God's love with those around us. As we respect and honor the uniqueness of each person, we will all grow in our understanding of ourselves as children of God.

In *The Learning Congregation: A New Vision of Leadership* (Westminster John Knox Press, 1997), Thomas R. Hawkins suggests that learning in the congregation should draw people out of personal space into community. In community we develop relationships of mutuality that express themselves in compassion and give us courage for action.

Hawkins' perspective provides us with an excellent reminder that Christian community and Christian fellowship are more than an "in-house mutual admiration society." In Christ we discover our connection to every other human being. Our relationships within the congregation provide a springboard for building healthy relationships in the global community in which we live.

The practices that we develop within a teaching/learning environment emerge from our identity and vision. They also provide us with concrete ways to live out our identity and move toward our vision. In Chapter 2, we explored the role of spiritual disciplines in developing a teacher's relationship with God. Our small groups should also practice the spiritual disciplines together.

In addition to specific spiritual disciplines, teachers can provide opportunities for group members to develop their skills in sharing their faith comfortably, listening carefully, resolving conflict, expressing feelings appropriately, and making decisions wisely. We employ each of these skills at various times in our families, at work, and in other settings. Our participation in congregational classes and small groups can provide us with direction in how to employ these skills in a way that is consistent with our vision of Christian discipleship.

Teachers serve as role models and guides for embodying the practices of our faith. We need to support and encourage our group members as we work together to develop the "holy habits" that lead to healthy relationships with God and neighbor.

A part of the content of any teaching/learning setting is a specific body of knowledge or information. Teachers and other educational leaders of children and youth may be responsible for selecting the topics that will be covered in a particular group. Adult classes usually participate in the decision-making process. Regardless of who decides what will be studied, teachers need to be knowledgeable of the overall content of the Christian faith in order to determine which issues and topics will help the group grow toward mature faith.

The basic building block of our content is the Bible. We need to be growing congregations that know and love God's Word. The wonderful thing about studying the Bible is that no matter how many times you've read or heard a passage of Scripture, you gain new insights every time you read it. As our experience changes and grows and as we mature, we discover fresh perspectives on what God is teaching us.

Basic Bible study should include an introduction to the entire Bible. Group members should become familiar with the major biblical people, the chronology of Israel's history, the life and ministry of Jesus, and the events that shaped the early church. Group members will benefit also from learning about how the Bible was developed—when and by whom various books were written, what circumstances the biblical characters were facing, and how the writer interpreted the action of God.

As people develop a basic grasp of the content of the Bible, teachers will want to challenge them to a more in-depth approach to Bible study. We can help people begin to identify themes that emerge from reading an entire book of the Bible, or from the prophets, and so forth. We might explore biblical concepts, such as grace and redemption.

Congregations need to provide intensive "laboratory" experiences for helping mature Christians continue to grow in faith and discipleship. Even at the most basic level, teachers should help group members discern God's Word for their lives. As people mature, this becomes a more significant part of group life. Teachers of these groups should be able to listen carefully, practice spiritual discernment, and promote dialogue.

In addition to the Bible, our group members' spiritual growth will be enhanced through knowledge of past and present Christian leaders. Those of us who are United Methodist will want our group members to be acquainted with John and Charles Wesley, Philip Otterbein, Francis Asbury, and other men and women who have shaped our United Methodist heritage. To fully understand the distinctiveness of our denomination, we must also be familiar with John Calvin, Martin Luther, and other Reformation leaders.

With the popularity in recent years of narrative theology, spiritual autobiographies or biographies have proved to be an effective vehicle for exploring diverse perspectives on faith. Many people have been rediscovering the Christian mystics, such as Julian of Norwich and Teresa of Ávila. Studying Karl Barth, Dietrich Bonhoeffer, and Reinhold and H. Richard Niebuhr will give us insights into critical theological thinkers from earlier in this century. We will also benefit from reading Thomas Merton, Howard Thurman, Martin Luther King, Jr., Dorothy Day, Mother Teresa, and others who have written from a faith perspective about the issues that face our world. Teachers who are familiar with what is available will be a great asset to their small group as they suggest possibilities for examining faith from another Christian's perspective.

Content includes a wide range of contemporary issues. Since our teaching and learning should result in the practical application of our faith to daily life, teachers should assist group members in exploring the implications of faith for addressing those issues. Issues will vary from place to place; however, it is hard to imagine that hunger, poverty, homelessness, racism, unemployment, access to quality education and healthcare, and other aspects of discrimination and inequity will be totally eliminated by the time this book is published. More than likely, at least one of these issues is affecting the lives of some of your congregation's members. Your small group will be wise to analyze these issues from a faith perspective and devise strategies for addressing them.

Content also includes stories, rituals, and symbols. It includes the religious language we use and the way we interpret religious experience. The stories we tell one another reflect our self-concept, purpose, and meaning. The practices that organize our common life in meaningful ways become rituals of celebration and affirmation. Symbols function in much the same way as metaphors: They point to a reality that exceeds our ability to define or describe. They stand for that which grounds our being in the holy. Teachers provide access to meaning-making for their group members when they offer opportunities to tell stories, explore symbols, and develop rituals.

# METHODOLOGY

Small-group leaders should choose teaching methods that are appropriate for the age level and learning preferences of their group members, that "break open" the content for exploration and reflection, and that are congruent with the kind of learning environment they are attempting to create. There are hundreds of teaching methods—many more than this book can possibly address. I have selected several categories of methods to highlight because of how they support the creation of sacred space. Each category can be dissected further into a variety of methods. But that is for another book.

## Conversation

In *The Learning Congregation: A New Vision of Leadership* (Westminster John Knox Press, 1997), Thomas R. Hawkins speculates that the key activity for congregational leaders may be to lead conversation. He postulates that dialogue, inquiry, and conversation are intricately related to the discernment of God's will for our lives. He proposes that effective dialogue is a balance between advocacy and inquiry. Advocacy represents our attempt to clearly articulate and promote understanding of our position on a particular issue. Inquiry represents our attempt to understand the perspectives of other group members.

Skills related to inquiry include soliciting feedback, identifying values and assumptions, and exploring potential actions. As we make explicit the reasoning behind our thinking, we gain deeper insight into what makes us tick. We can also challenge our own assumptions and consider new options. Inquiry increases the possibility of developing shared meaning with the group.

Teachers can help their group members develop skills in inquiry and dialogue, such as those described in Chapter 3. Paraphrasing and asking open-ended questions are two of the skills that facilitate dialogue. As we continue to build places of safety, respect, and trust, we can discuss our opinions while respecting the opinions of others. We will eliminate defensiveness and fear as we foster honesty and the willingness to be vulnerable.

## Storytelling

Storytelling is a powerful method for Christian formation. According to Richard Robert Osmer, personal identity most frequently takes a narrative shape (*Teaching for Faith: A Guide for Teachers of Adult Classes*; Westminster John Knox Press, 1992). Storytelling is one way in which we share our faith. As our group members tell personal stories, the events and people that shaped their self-perception will emerge. The Christian story helps us reinterpret our personal stories in light of the gospel.

Osmer suggests a five-step process for storytelling:

- remembering—recalling important parts of our life stories that relate to the focus of the group session;
- reflecting—taking a step back from our lives to see what patterns and themes are emerging;
- encountering—engaging some aspect of the Christian story;
- sharing—disclosing parts of our stories that we usually choose to hide from others;
- deciding—choosing how we will live differently in light of our new understandings of who we are.

Storytelling serves to identify the interpretive frameworks out of which we live each day. The stories we choose to tell name how we perceive ourselves in relation to others and to God. Since our interpretive frameworks are primarily subconscious, it can be a painful process to recognize them. It can also be a liberating process.

Roberta C. Bondi is a phenomenal example of this kind of story-teller. In books such as *Memories of God: Theological Reflections on a Life* (Abingdon Press, 1995) and *In Ordinary Time: Healing the Wounds of the Heart* (Abingdon Press, 1996), she tells stories of her childhood that shaped her perception of God. These early experiences distanced her from a God who, she felt sure, could never love her. The power of Dr. Bondi's stories lies in their ability to illuminate the realities of our own experience, to get in touch with the stories that have shaped our concept of God and how God relates to us. This kind of storytelling leads to deeper commitment to God and to newer, more authentic perceptions of ourselves.

## Team Learning

Team learning actually involves a set of five processes. Karen E. Watkins and Victoria J. Marsick describe these processes in their book, *Sculpting the Learning Organization: Lessons in the Art and Science of Systemic Change* (Jossey-Bass Publishers, 1993). The processes include the following:

### 1. FRAMING

Have you ever been in a conversation and afterwards wondered if you were even in the same room with the other person? Our different perspectives may cause us to talk past each other. Just as we frame a picture, we "frame" our initial perceptions of an issue, situation, person, or object, based on past understanding and present input. We use assumptions and mental models to filter our experience, focusing on one aspect and ignoring another.

### 2. REFRAMING

This involves a process of transforming our perception into a new understanding or frame. We recognize that other people are framing a situation differently than we are. As we identify our own frame, we can learn to view a situation from multiple perspectives.

Here's a story to illustrate the first two steps in the process. In 1978 my husband and I lived in San Antonio, Texas, where there are a number of military bases. At Thanksgiving the church in which I was working sponsored an "invite-a-serviceman-to-dinner" program. I began to imagine some young man or woman of eighteen or nineteen away from home for the first time, lonely and depressed at the thought of eating Thanksgiving dinner in a mess hall. I thought it would be a terrific idea for Steve and me to open our home to one of those lonely young people. So one night I said, "I thought I would invite someone in the military to eat with us on Thanksgiving."

How did Steve respond? I might as well have suggested that I cut up our first-born offspring and serve her for dinner! You see, Steve heard what I said and immediately imagined a fifty-year-old veteran of the military who would have nothing in common with two young adults. Since he was in school at the time and I worked on weekends, we often went several days without spending much time with each other. So a part of Steve's frame was anticipation of spending time with me during the extended Thanksgiving holidays. Therefore, he "heard" me stomp all over his plans (which were unarticulated up to that point) and "tell" him I'd rather spend time with a stranger than with him.

We had some major reframing to do! So it is in our small groups. We assume that what we tell someone is heard and understood in the same way we meant it. But, of course, that is frequently not true. Teachers serve their group members well when they help them articulate their assumptions and be open to different perspectives.

### 3. INTEGRATING PERSPECTIVES

Our communities of faith would not grow much if we simply "dumped" our opinions on one another and left them sitting out there flapping in the breeze. We learn and grow as we synthesize diverse experiences and perspectives. Synthesis also encompasses resolution of apparent conflicts without compromise or majority rule. Christian community does not operate in a "may-the-best-man-win" mentality.

Thomas Hawkins, building on Watkins and Marsick's work, suggests that there are two phases of integration: dialogue and discussion. We use dialogue to explore an issue, to examine differing opinions, and to recognize alternatives. We use discussion to come to consensus and make decisions. Hawkins believes that teachers and small-group leaders facilitate group process when they help identify which of the phases of integration the group is using. This clarifies direction and diminishes confusion.

### 4. EXPERIMENTING

We experiment when we try a new behavior or plan a new action. This is risky business and places us in a vulnerable position. Yet the kind of Christian community we have been talking about in this book supports people in their experimentation. Under the right circumstances, we learn from our mistakes as well as from our successes. As we imagine new possibilities, we experiment with ways to make the possibility a reality. In the process we discover new abilities and new knowledge that reinforce or reshape our perspectives.

### 5. CROSSING BOUNDARIES

Many of the formal structures in our congregations unintentionally create unnecessary (and invisible) boundaries that inhibit growth and interaction throughout the congregation. Team learning happens when we eliminate intangible barriers that separate person from person in order to work and learn together.

In a business, crossing boundaries happens when production staff work with advertising staff to market a product that will be appealing to consumers. In an educational institution, crossing boundaries happens when administrators, parents, and teachers work together to revise the curriculum. In a congregation, crossing boundaries happens when members of missions, education, and stewardship ministry teams cosponsor a learning fair, focusing on opportunities for service locally and globally.

## Creative Arts

The use of art, drama, dance, and music addresses the effective dimension of our personality and helps us use our spatial (visual) and bodily-kinesthetic intelligences. We can express emotion and explore alternatives in non-threatening ways. The arts put us in touch with our own creativity, which reflects the creativity of God; and they foster imagination, which is instrumental in envisioning new possibilities for the future.

Teachers who are planning to incorporate the creative arts in a group session will need to estimate as accurately as possible how much time is needed for the activity. The arts may require special equipment or supplies (compact disk player, paint, paintbrushes, water, paper towels, and so forth).

Teachers should also consider inviting a guest instructor to lead the group in activities that the teacher cannot lead. For example, a liturgical dancer can meet with a group as they study worship. As a part of the learning activities, group members can express their praise of God through dance, under the direction of the experienced dancer.

## Resources

Another component of the teaching/learning dynamic is resources. Most often we think of curriculum resources. Our denomination has a wide range of printed materials that facilitate study, reflection, and application. They are suitable for use in Sunday school classes, retreat settings, camping experiences, and weekday small groups.

In addition to these resources, teachers can use media resources to support group members' learning. We will want to be aware of contemporary films and songs that provide fruitful discussion of the issues facing our society today. There are television programs, often sponsored by public television stations, that reflect religious themes, such as Bill Moyers' series of programs on Genesis. The Odyssey channel on cable television schedules several programs related to The United Methodist Church. Check your local television guide to determine what is available in your area. (Remember to check licensing requirements for videos and other media resources you use in a teaching/learning setting.)

Increasingly, computers and the Internet are becoming resources for our teaching and learning. There are CD-ROMs that contain a great deal of information about the Bible. The American Bible Society is one source for these resources. We can also use e-mail and the World Wide Web to correspond with Christians around the world, to see some of our mission sites, and to discuss issues that are facing the church in our community and in other places.

We should not forget human resources as we plan for teaching and learning. Earlier I suggested inviting a liturgical dancer to incorporate the arts into a group. We also can invite guests to make presentations about issues in our community, about United Methodist mission around the world, or about personal issues, such as handling stress.

This book cannot provide an exhaustive list of available resources. What is important here is that teachers are clear about their teaching goals and are knowledgeable about the resources available to help them reach their goals. These goals should be developed in cooperation with our group members, as together we seek to grow in God's grace.

## CONCLUSION

Teaching and learning for Christian discipleship is an awesome task. It is a means of God's grace that leads to an ever-deepening commitment to the love of God and love of neighbor.

I believe that God is calling us to build new systems for teaching and learning that are adequate for meeting the challenges of today. Our God is a mighty God! What God calls us to do, God equips us to achieve.

When we gather in Christian community, the risen Christ is in our midst. As we experience God's transforming presence, we testify to the power of God's redemptive love. Like the blind man whom Jesus healed, we proclaim: "I may not know everything there is to know about who Jesus is, but I'm learning! And this one thing I do know—I once was blind, but now I see!" (John 9:25, paraphrased).

May God give us eyes to see God, ears to hear God, and hearts to love God and God's people. And may the grace of our Lord Jesus Christ be with us all.

# GUIDE FOR GROUP USE

1. Discuss how teaching is a means of experiencing God's grace. You may want to use illustrations from your experience. Talk about how teaching and learning in your congregation currently fosters a recognition of God's transforming presence.

2. Make a list of the ways in which your congregation builds corporate memory and supports the development of Christian identity. Evaluate which of these is most effective. How do you know? What do you need to do differently?

3. Review the biblical and contemporary metaphors on page 89. Which of these metaphors speaks to you? What other metaphors and images represent your congregation's vision for the world? How does your teaching and learning form that vision? How is your teaching and learning informed by that vision? How does your vision shape your group members' Christian identity?

4. Provide resources or workshops for teachers to explore the theory of multiple intelligences. Follow up with teachers to discover how they determine their group members' learning preference, how they are effectively using a variety of learning approaches, and how you might continue to support them.

5. Take a survey of your teachers to collect data related to teaching methods used in your small groups. Provide opportunities for teachers to develop skills in using new methods and in selecting methods appropriate for their group members.

# BIBLIOGRAPHY

### Starting and Maintaining Small-Group Ministries

*The Big Book on Small Groups*, by Jeffrey Arnold (InterVarsity Press, 1992).

*Gathering the Seekers: Spiritual Growth Through Small Group Ministry*, by James R. Newby (The Alban Institute, 1995).

*Good Things Happen: Experiencing Community in Small Groups*, by Dick Westley (Twenty-Third Publications, 1992).

*Leading Small Groups: Basic Skills for Church and Community Organizations*, by Nathan W. Turner (Judson Press, 1997).

*Life Together*, by Dietrich Bonhoeffer (HarperCollins, Publishers, Inc., 1978).

*One Anothering: Biblical Building Blocks for Small Groups*, by Richard C. Meyer (Innisfree Press, 1990).

*Planning for Christian Education: A Practical Guide for Your Congregation*, edited by Carol F. Krau (Discipleship Resources, 1994).

*Prepare Your Church for the Future*, by Carl F. George (Chosen Books Publishing Company, 1991).

*Sharing the Journey: Support Groups and America's New Quest for Community*, by Robert Wuthnow (The Free Press, 1996).

*The Small Group Book: The Practical Guide for Nurturing Christians and Building Churches*, by Dale Galloway and Kathi Mills (Fleming H. Revell Company, 1995).

*Small Group Idea Book: Resources to Enrich Community, Worship and Prayer, Nurture and Outreach*, edited by Cindy Bunch (InterVarsity Press, 1996).

*Small Group Ministry with Youth*, by David R. Veerman (Chariot Victor Publishing, 1992). [Out of print. Check your church or local library.]

*Small Groups: Getting Started*, by Suzanne G. Braden and Shirley F. Clement (Discipleship Resources, 1989).

*Small Groups in the Church: A Handbook for Creating Community*, by Thomas G. Kirkpatrick (The Alban Institute, 1995).

*Starting Small Groups and Keeping Them Going* (Augsburg Fortress Publishers, 1995).

*Starting Small Groups: Building Communities That Matter* (part of the Leadership Insight series), by Jeffrey Arnold, edited by Herb Miller (Abingdon Press, 1997).

*StartUp! Preparing to Lead Your Small Group* (part of the YouthSearch series), by Don Hackett (Abingdon Press, 1995). [Out of print. Check your church or local library.]

*Successful Home Cell Groups*, by David Y. Cho and Harold Hostetler (Logos Publishers, 1987).

*Way to Grow: Dynamic Church Growth Through Small Groups*, by Ronald J. Lavin (CSS Publishing Company, 1996).

*Where Do We Go From Here? A Guidebook for the Cell Group Church*, by Ralph W. Neighbour, Jr. (Touch Publications, Inc., 1990).

## Accountability Groups

*Class Leaders: Recovering a Tradition*, by David Lowes Watson (Discipleship Resources, 1991).

*Covenant Discipleship: Christian Formation Through Mutual Accountability*, by David Lowes Watson (Discipleship Resources, 1991).

*The Early Methodist Class Meeting: Its Origins and Significance*, by David Lowes Watson (Discipleship Resources, 1985).

*Forming Christian Disciples: The Role of Covenant Discipleship and Class Leaders in the Congregation*, by David Lowes Watson (Discipleship Resources, 1995).

*Practicing Our Faith: A Way of Life for a Searching People*, edited by Dorothy C. Bass (Jossey-Bass Publishers, Incorporated, 1997).

*Sprouts: Nurturing Children through Covenant Discipleship*, by Edie Genung Harris and Shirley L. Ramsey (Discipleship Resources, 1996).

*Wesley and the Quadrilateral: Renewing the Conversation*, edited by W. Stephen Gunter (Abingdon Press, 1997).

## Justice Issues/Ministry in Daily Life

*The Company of Strangers: Christians and the Renewal of America's Public Life*, by Parker J. Palmer and Martin E. Marty (Crossroad Publishing Co., 1983).

*Good News to the Poor: John Wesley's Evangelical Economics*, by Theodore W. Jennings (Abingdon Press, 1990).

*In Search of Faithfulness: Lessons From the Christian Community*, by William E. Diehl (Fortress Press, 1987). [Out of print. Check your church or local library.]

John Wesley's Social Ethics: Praxis and Principles, by Manfred Marquardt; translated by W. Stephen Gunter and John E. Steely (Abingdon Press, 1992). [Out of print. Check your church or local library.]

Living Our Beliefs: The United Methodist Way, by Bishop Kenneth L. Carder (Discipleship Resources, 1996).

Ministry in Daily Life: A Practical Guide for Congregations, by William E. Diehl (The Alban Institute, 1996).

## Spiritual Disciplines

Celebration of Discipline: The Path to Spiritual Growth, by Richard J. Foster (HarperCollins, Publishers, Inc., 1988).

Communion, Community, Commonweal: Readings for Spiritual Leadership, edited by John S. Mogabgab (Upper Room Books, 1995).

Connecting to God: Nurturing Spirituality Through Small Groups, by Corinne Ware (The Alban Institute, 1997).

Devotional Life in the Wesleyan Tradition, by Steve Harper (Upper Room Books, 1983).

Discover Your Spiritual Type: A Guide to Individual and Congregational Growth, by Corinne Ware (The Alban Institute, 1995).

A History of Christian Spirituality: An Analytical Introduction, by Urban T. Holmes (HarperCollins, 1981). [Out of print. Check your church or local library.]

Invitation to Presence: A Guide to Spiritual Disciplines, by Wendy Miller (Upper Room Books, 1995).

The Presence of God in the Christian Life: John Wesley and the Means of Grace, by Henry H. Knight III (Scarecrow Press, Incorporated, 1992).

Soul Feast: An Invitation to the Christian Spiritual Life, by Marjorie J. Thompson (Westminster John Knox Press, 1995).

Spiritual Life: The Foundation for Preaching and Teaching, by John H. Westerhoff (Westminster John Knox Press, 1994).

Transforming Bible Study: A Leader's Guide, by Walter Wink (Abingdon Press, 1990).

## Spiritual Leadership

Knowing Me, Knowing God: Exploring Your Spirituality with Myers-Briggs, by Malcom Goldsmith (Abingdon Press, 1997).

*Learning to Listen: A Guide for Spiritual Friends*, by Wendy Miller (Upper Room Books, 1993).

*Listening and Caring Skills in Ministry: A Guide for Pastors, Counselors, and Small Group Leaders*, by John S. Savage (Abingdon Press, 1996).

*Personality Type and Religious Leadership*, by Roy M. Oswald and Otto Kroeger (The Alban Institute, 1988).

*The Radical Wesley and Patterns for Church Renewal*, by Howard A. Snyder (Wipf & Stock Publishers, 1996).

## Systems

*The Fifth Discipline: The Art and Practice of the Learning Organization*, by Peter M. Senge (Currency/Doubleday, 1994).

*Healthy Congregations: A Systems Approach*, by Peter L. Steinke (The Alban Institute, 1996).

*How Your Church Family Works: Understanding Congregations as Emotional Systems*, by Peter L. Steinke (The Alban Institute, 1993).

*Leadership and the New Science: Learning About Organization From an Orderly Universe*, by Margaret J. Wheatley (Berrett/Koehler Publishers, 1994).

*Leading Change in the Congregation: Spiritual and Organizational Tools for Leaders*, by Gilbert R. Rendle (The Alban Institute, 1997).

*The Learning Congregation: A New Vision of Leadership*, by Thomas R. Hawkins (Westminster John Knox Press, 1997).

*The Once and Future Church: Reinventing the Congregation for a New Mission Frontier*, by Loren B. Mead (The Alban Institute, 1993).

*Quest for Quality in the Church: A New Paradigm*, by Ezra Earl Jones (Discipleship Resources, 1993).

*Sculpting the Learning Organization: Lessons in the Art and Science of Systemic Change*, by Karen E. Watkins and Victoria J. Marsick (Jossey-Bass Publishers, 1993).

*Systemic Religious Education*, by Timothy Arthur Lines (Religious Education Press, 1987).

*Understanding Your Congregation as a System: Congregational Systems Inventory*, by George Parsons and Speed B. Leas (The Alban Institute, 1993). [Out of print. Check your church or local library.]

*Understanding Your Congregation as a System: The Manual*, by George D. Parsons and Speed B. Leas (The Alban Institute, 1994).

## Teaching, Learning, and Leading

*Becoming a Thinking Christian*, by John B. Cobb, Jr. (Abingdon Press, 1993).

*The Big Little School: 200 Years of the Sunday School*, by Robert W. Lynn and Elliott Wright (Abingdon Press, 1980). [Out of print. Check your church or local library.]

*By What Authority: A Conversation on Teaching Among United Methodists*, edited by Elizabeth Box Price and Charles R. Foster (Abingdon Press, 1991).

*Educating Congregations: The Future of Christian Education*, by Charles R. Foster (Abingdon Press, 1994).

*Foundations: Shaping the Ministry of Christian Education in Your Congregation* (Discipleship Resources, 1993).

*Frames of Mind: The Theory of Multiple Intelligences*, by Howard Gardner (BasicBooks, 1983).

*Gifts Differing: Understanding Personality Type*, by Isabel Briggs Myers (Consulting Psychologists Press, 1995).

*Mapping Christian Education: Approaches to Congregational Learning*, edited by Jack L. Seymour (Abingdon Press, 1997).

*7 Kinds of Smart: Identifying and Developing Your Many Intelligences*, by Thomas Armstrong (Plume, 1993).

*7 Ways of Teaching the Bible to Children*, by Barbara Bruce (Abingdon Press, 1996).

*Sharing Faith: A Comprehensive Approach to Religious Education and Pastoral Ministry*, by Thomas H. Groome (Harper San Francisco, 1991). [Out of print. Check your church or local library.]

*Spiritual Awakening: A Guide to Spiritual Life in Congregations*, by John Ackerman (The Alban Institute, 1994).

*Teaching and Learning in Communities of Faith: Empowering Adults Through Religious Education*, by Linda J. Vogel (Jossey-Bass Publishers, 1991).

*Teaching for Faith: A Guide for Teachers of Adult Classes*, by Richard Robert Osmer (Westminster John Knox Press, 1992).

*Teaching from the Heart: Theology and Educational Method*, by Mary Elizabeth Moore (Trinity Press International, 1998).

*Teaching Godly Play: The Sunday Morning Handbook*, by Jerome W. Berryman (Abingdon Press, 1995).

*Thinking the Faith: Christian Theology in a North American Context*, by Douglas John Hall (Fortress Press, 1991).

*Using the Bible in Groups*, by Roberta Hestenes (Westminster John Knox Press, 1985).

## Devotional Reading

*Alive Now*, bi-monthly magazine (The Upper Room).

*The Carpenter and The Unbuilder: Stories for the Spiritual Quest*, by David M. Griebner and Michael Williams (Upper Room Books, 1996).

*Devotional Classics: Selected Readings for Individuals and Groups*, edited by Richard J. Foster and James Bryan Smith (Harper San Francisco, 1993).

*The Grand Sweep: 365 Days from Genesis Through Revelation—A Bible Study for Individuals and Groups*, by J. Ellsworth Kalas (Abingdon Press, 1996).

*In Ordinary Time: Healing the Wounds of the Heart*, by Roberta C. Bondi (Abingdon Press, 1996).

*Making All Things New: An Invitation to the Spiritual Life*, by Henri J. M. Nouwen (HarperCollins, Publishers, Inc., 1981).

*Memories of God: Theological Reflections on a Life*, by Roberta C. Bondi (Abingdon Press, 1995).

*Searching for Shalom: Reasons for Creative Worship*, by Ann Weems (Westminster John Knox Press, 1991).

*The Upper Room Disciplines*, 1999, edited by Rita Collett (Upper Room Books, 1998).